ONCE A COWBOY

ONCE A COWBOY

WALT GARRISON

WITH JOHN TULLIUS

RANDOM HOUSE NEW YORK

Library of Congress Cataloging-in-Publication Data

Garrison, Walt.
Once a cowboy / by Walt Garrison and John Tullius.
p. cm.
ISBN 0-394-57685-3
1. Garrison, Walt. 2. Football players—United States—Biography.
3. Dallas Cowboys (Football team) 4. Cowboys—United States-
-Biography. I. Tullius, John. II. Title.
GV939.G35A3 1988
796.332'092'4--dc19
[B]   88-18240
CIP
Manufactured in the United States of America
24689753
First Edition

TO MY MOM AND DAD, MUTT AND ANN GARRISON, WHO SACRI-
FICED SO MUCH SO EACH OF US KIDS COULD HAVE A LITTLE.

TO MY SONS, MARTY AND BEN, WHO DON'T REMEMBER SEEING
ME PLAY. I'M NOT SURE THEY MISSED MUCH. I LOVE THEM BOTH
VERY MUCH.

TO BILL ROBINSON, WHO WILL LIVE FOREVER IN MY MEMORY.
HE WAS A GOOD FRIEND. I MISS HIM.

FOREWORD
BY DAN REEVES

Walt Garrison has always had a reputation for speaking his mind and that's just what he does in this book. He tells exactly what it was like to play for the Dallas Cowboys during their "golden era." In the late sixties and seventies Dallas played in five Super Bowls and Walt was there for most of it. He froze his behind off at the "Ice Bowl" against Green Bay in 1967 and he was there when we won the world championship at the Super Bowl against Miami in 1972.

But Walt's focus in this book is not really on the games he played but the people who played the games. There's Landry and Lilly, Meredith and Ditka, Namath and Butkus and Payton and O.J. And even a little bit of Dan Reeves in there. A whole cast of interesting and hilarious characters brought to life by one of the greatest storytellers ever to play the game of football.

Walt could always spin a heck of a yarn. The *Dallas Morning News* called him "Pro football's Will Rogers." Walt was always brimming over with anecdotes and limericks and jokes and stories and songs. At the drop of a hat he'd be reciting poetry. He was hilarious.

Walt loved to have a good time and, believe me, I shared a lot of those good times with him—as you'll read in this book. But when it came time to play, Walt was ready. Man, was he ready!

The stories about how tough Walt Garrison was are football legends. I've been in professional football as a player and coach since 1965 and I've never seen anybody as tough as Walt. He never backed off from anyone or anything. And his capacity to take pain was unbelievable.

In the conference championship game in 1970 against San Francisco, Walt played with a broken collarbone and a couple of broken ribs. In the second quarter he broke his ankle. They took him in and shot his ankle with Novocaine and he went back out and played the entire second half. He even caught the touchdown pass that iced the game for us. That was the most incredible show of guts I've ever seen on a football field.

That game epitomized Walt Garrison.

Actually, because Walt was so tough, his accomplishments were often overlooked. He scored thirty touchdowns and gained almost 4000 yards and almost every inch of that came in the last five years of his career after Walt took over the starting fullback position when Don Perkins retired.

Walt didn't have blazing speed like Simpson or the dazzling moves of Walter Payton. And he certainly wasn't very big. But he could get the yardage you needed, when you needed it.

Walt had a great body lean and his legs never stopped moving. All a defensive man ever saw was helmet, shoulder pads and knees. He would hit and spin and turn and twist and keep on going until they stopped him. He wasn't a great run-to-daylight-type back. He was a guy who made daylight.

If there wasn't a hole, he'd hit the guy and knock him off, spin and keep running.

Again, it was his toughness that made him a great player.

But, of course, football was not all Walt was known for. Dallas billed him as "the Cowboys' Cowboy." Rodeo and whittling and dippin snuff. And it wasn't just a lot of PR. Walt was known as one of the top bulldoggers on the professional rodeo circuit.

Ya, Walt Garrison is a cowboy. His values and his way of living are right out of the old West. He's tough and durable and he tells it straight. There is nothing phony about Walt Garrison. If he doesn't like you, you know it. But if he does like you, there isn't anything he won't do for you.

Walt and I have been best of friends since the first day we met. And it's one of those friendships that'll never end. But, heck, Walt is an easy guy to like. He's honest and intelligent, funny and entertaining.

Exactly like his book.

ACKNOWLEDGMENTS

DAN REEVES

KENT CLARK

DAVE MANDERS

LEE ROY JORDAN

CHARLIE WATERS

CLIFF HARRIS

PAT TOOMAY

BOB LOOMIS

D. D. LEWIS

DAVE EDWARDS

DON TALBERT

ERNEST OWEN

WALTER HARVEY

B. F. PHILLIPS, JR.

AND ALL THE PLAYERS, COACHES, MEDIA, AND
FRONT-OFFICE PEOPLE I HAD THE PLEASURE OF BEING
AROUND FOR NINE YEARS

AND A SPECIAL THANKS TO MY WIFE, DEBBIE,
WHO HAS MADE OUR LIVES A JOY TO LIVE

CONTENTS

PART THREE: WINNING THE BIG ONE

PART ONE

 ROOKIE

CHAPTER ONE

LITTLE PUDDIN

Before I was drafted by the Dallas Cowboys in 1966 they had never made the playoffs. In fact, they had never even had a winning season. After I joined the team we made the playoffs eight straight years and never had a losing season for twenty years! That's what a slow, underweight, fifth-round draft choice from Oklahoma State can do for a team.

Even with all that promise, I still had a lot to learn when I hit the pro game. When you're a rookie, you're about as dumb as a steer at an orgy. Not only don't you know the plays and the players, you're not all that filled in on life either. So you tend to make a big fool of yourself just about every chance you get.

The first week I joined the Cowboys I didn't know nothin. They let me run the ball every once in a while but mostly, like every other rookie, I spent most of my time on the kamikaze squads covering kicks.

So one day I'm lining up for a punt-coverage team and Bob Lilly lines up over me. My assignment is to fire out, hit the guy, stop him, release, run down the field 40 or 50 yards, turn around and block the same guy.

So the first play I fire out and Pow! I hit Lilly a good one. Then, Pew! down the field I go and here comes Lilly lumbering along. And I run up and Wham! I give him another good shot. And as I'm trotting back to run the play again I'm thinking, "Bob Lilly—All-Pro my ass! I could kill him if I wanted to."

Next play we run the same thing. Lilly lines up over me and I say to myself, "I'm gonna get him good. I'm gonna really nail him this time. He'll respect me when this is over." So I start to fire out and Lilly just reaches his big paw out and gives me a head slap and the next thing I know I'm flat on my back and Lilly takes off running down the field.

That pissed me off. I'm thinking, "You big son of a bitch. I'm gonna get you for that." So I jump up and take off after Lilly. When I catch him I'm gonna drop him like a sack of spuds. Lilly's got a 2- or 3-yard lead but I'm a running back and Lilly's nothing but a big slow lineman. So I take off and I'm pumping as hard as I can and I can't catch him. He outruns me! When we get down to the other end of the field, Lilly's 10 yards in front of me. I couldn't have blocked him if I'd wanted to.

That was my introduction to Mr. Lilly.

The first time I ever touched the ball in a professional football game I ran for 65 yards. That was against the Detroit Lions in my first exhibition game my rookie year and I remember thinking to myself as I crossed the goal line, "Hey, this pro football is easy. Heck, it might take me two, three weeks to learn this game."

That turned out to be the longest run I ever had in nine years of pro football. I also gained 165 yards that day and that was the most yards I ever ran for in my career. I was playing behind the great Don Perkins who now sits in Dallas's Ring of Honor. But I could see it wasn't going to take me long to put the old fart on the bench where he belonged. I'd missed the first two preseason games because I played in the College All-Star game. But when I showed up I played an entire half my first game back and the next week I played another half. I thought, "Man, this is great. I'm going to play a whole bunch. I can't wait for the season to start." And when it did, I never played again. In fact, I didn't play for three years except in the last few minutes of a game when we were ahead by 30 or 40 points.

"OK, Walt, get in there. You can't hurt us."

I had a few lessons to learn off the field too. When I first came to the Cowboys we used to have our training facility over off the Central Expressway. It wasn't exactly plush. The players' dressing room was an old sheet-metal building that was like an oven in the summer. The lockers were nothing but A-frame stalls with wooden pegs sticking out of the wall to hang your clothes on.

But, you know, I thought I'd entered heaven the first day I walked into that beat-up old tin can. There was Dandy Don Meredith and Bullet Bob Hayes and Lee Roy "Killer" Jordan—guys you read about. They weren't teammates, they were legends. So I wandered starry-eyed into the dressing room that day and eventually found my way over to the equipment counter where they handed me a roll of stuff—T-shirt, socks and jock.

Jack Eskridge, the equipment manager, said, "Here's your gear, Walt. Your locker's right around yonder." And he pointed off in the general direction where my locker was supposed to be.

So I walk over there looking for my name up on one of the stalls and there was Pete Gent sitting on a stool in front of one of the lockers. Gent was the renegade who wrote the blockbuster best seller *North Dallas Forty.* He was a weirdo from the opening kickoff. But he was a funny guy. My favorite Gent line was, "A paranoid is a guy with all the facts."

Anyway, Pete was sitting next to an old metal I-beam post that held the building up and it's got my name taped to it. And there's my shoes and shoulder pads and everything stacked up on the floor next to this metal post.

"Hey, Walt," Pete said, "looks like you didn't get a locker. They just don't have room for everybody. So you'll have to wait until they cut some of these other guys around here and one'll open up. But look, in the meantime I got two lockers here so I'll let you hang your clothes in one. But don't you put any of your old sweaty stuff in there. And no goddamn muddy shoes either!"

It took me a whole week to find out that Pete didn't really have two lockers. One of them was mine. And I never did figure it out for myself. Somebody had to tell me. That's how dumb I was. After a while Pete finally said, "Oh, hell, Walt, you can have this locker!"

"Hey, thanks, Pete," I said. What a nice guy. People were tripping over my stuff and kicking it all over the place and I was glad to get it off that floor. So I went up to Jack Eskridge again and told him, "I won't be needing a locker because Gent give me one of his." And Jack started laughing. "Hell, that was your locker all the time."

And I thought to myself, "Why, you stupid hick."

When you're a rookie you take all the crap the veterans can dish out. You're on the bottom of a very rigid pecking order and you find out right away you're the chicken with the little pecker.

We were eating dinner one night at training camp and a rookie asked Dave Edwards, nice as can be, would he please pass the potatoes. And without looking up Edwards grunted, "Eat something down there by you."

One of the big laughs at training camp was to send a rookie down to the pizza parlor to pick up a pizza at ten minutes to eleven. Curfew was eleven. "Run down to Orlando's and get me a pizza. Here's the money. Go." There ain't no way they could get to Orlando's and be back by eleven o'clock. When they'd come back huffin and puffin at quarter after, the coaches would hang a $100 fine on them for breaking curfew and we'd get our pizza.

A rookie doesn't even get respect from the trainers. Because they were so busy during training camp, Don Cochrane and Larry Gardner, the two Cowboy trainers, were forced to give rookies the hurry-up tape job. After you became a veteran, they'd tape you up good. But when you're talking about taping eighty rookies twice a day, and at least seventy-five of them you're never going to see when the regular season begins, hell, they're lucky they got taped at all.

But a rookie would gladly put up with all the dirty tricks, all the shit details, all the blister tape jobs if he could just avoid "The Call." That's what we used to call it—The Call. Coach Myers, the offensive-line coach, would call and tell you, "Coach Landry wants to see you. Bring your playbook."

Myers was the hatchet man and he didn't get the job because he was a diplomat. He never wasted a lot of words and he never tried to ease you into it. "Garrison, get your playbook. Coach Landry wants to see you." And when he called, your blood ran cold. We called him "the Turk." That's the hatchet man on the Cowboys—the guy who cuts off your head in training camp. When the Turk made the call, you knew you were a memory.

In practice somebody'd say, "Hey, where's what's his name?"

"The Turk got him."

Myers always made the call after evening practice, right before dinner. The rest of the players went to supper and the victim was held in Coach Landry's office until everyone was in the dining room. And when you came back from eating the guy was gone. It was like he'd never been there. He was vaporized.

It was brutally efficient. The victim would go to Coach Landry's room. Landry would take the playbook from him and explain why they were cutting him. ("Hey, you're lousy. What can I say?") Then they'd tell him to go get his things. They'd already have his plane reservation made and they had some kids from the college who drove people to the airport, and just like that, the poor guy'd be off to LAX.

But there was a merciful reason for this disappearing act. Coach Landry felt that if the victim didn't have to face the other players it was a relief. You aren't feeling very good right about then. So it's a lot better than walking into the locker room and everybody saying, "Hey, what'd Landry say?"

"He cut my ass."

"Ah, too bad. Can I have your locker?"

Some of the veterans used to make the call to the rookies just for a little joke. "This is Jim Myers. Get your playbook. Coach Landry wants to see you." And you *knew* it was over. Then they'd start laughing. Or sometimes they'd let you go all the way over to Landry's office.

"Did you wanna see me, Coach?"

"No, get outta here. We're busy."

And they'd laugh when you got back. But it was hard to get mad because you were so happy you didn't get cut, hell, you wanted to kiss them.

It's hard for a rookie to get to know anybody. And a lot of that is the Turk's fault. Until you make the team, until you contribute, the veterans don't usually go out of their way to get to know you. As a rookie you just can't understand it. But when I was a veteran I knew exactly why. I tried not to get too close to any rookies because they'd be gone overnight. The life of a rookie is high risk. They've got the life expectancy of a fruit fly when the birds are feeding.

My first year in training camp I hung out with the other rookies, of course, and to this day I couldn't tell you their names, they came and went so fast. First of all, you don't have much time to socialize as it is in training camp. I studied my playbook when I wasn't eating or sleeping. Plus, I got there two weeks late because I played in the College All-Star game so I missed all of rookie camp and two weeks of regular training camp.

Actually, showing up late probably helped me make the team because the players who play in the All-Star game are not counted in the roster for the final cuts until two weeks after the deadline. That means you can get another chance to impress the coaches. Charlie Waters actually got cut in his rookie training camp but because he'd played in the All-Star game he didn't count on the official roster. Only the coaching staff had forgotten that. And when they realized what they'd done, they called him back. After that Charlie impressed them so much they kept him and he turned out to be an All-Pro. Don't tell me there ain't no luck in football.

So Charlie Waters is the only guy I ever knew who got the call from the Turk and survived.

Another thing that happens to all rookies is they get a nickname. All the players on the Cowboys had nicknames. Jethro Pugh was "Buzzard" because he was tall and skinny and his shoulders hunched up like a buzzard. "Sweet Lips" was Cornell Green because he could talk so fast you couldn't understand him, especially when he was drinking beer. Dan Reeves was "Frog" because he had a funny little stance with his rear end down real low just like a frog. There was Ralph "Rotten" Neely and John Niland was "Gorgo" named after the cartoon character "Gorgo the frog that ate New York" because Niland ate all the time. He ate everything in sight. The problem was the Cowboys had a weight limit and if you were over your limit, they'd fine you a hundred bucks a pound. They weighed you once a week. If you were two pounds over, it'd cost you $200. The next week if you were still two pounds over, they'd fine you $400.

But Niland was a smart *hombre*. Just before the weigh-in he'd order four or five extra-large pizzas delivered to his room. Then he'd go off to the weigh-in and he'd no sooner get off that scale than he'd be back in his room gorging on those tomato pies. The only problem was he'd have to throw it all up so he could pass the weigh-in the next week. Oh, that Niland was a sick boy!

Then there was Craig Baynam. He was a very religious guy. Since then he's fallen off the religion wagon with a vengeance. But back in those days he was a Bible-totin fool. Anyway, each week they had about thirty footballs they wanted you to sign that went to different organizations or individuals. They'd pay you like ten cents a ball. And the equipment man would check each ball and then check off your name against the team roster and tally up your dimes. Hey, it was beer money.

Well, anyway, Baynam used to sign the footballs "Craig Baynam—John 1:12" which was a favorite verse in scripture of his. So his nickname became "John One Dozen."

The only guy who didn't have a nickname was Bob Lilly. Lilly was too big for anybody to start calling him names. They called him "The Purple Cloud" at TCU because the Horned Frogs wore purple and Lilly was everywhere on that field. But at Dallas they just called him Mr. Lilly.

They called me "Puddin." That was the nickname Meredith hung on me. If I was picking a nickname I wouldn't have chosen the one I got. But a rookie didn't get to come in and give himself a nickname like "Flash" or "Great hands." It was always a veteran tagging a rookie with some label. Well, I'll tell you, I didn't exactly like Puddin and when you hear how I got that handle, you'll know why.

The night before the last game of my rookie season I was laying up in my hotel room and Meredith called me up and said, "Walt, what're you doin for supper tonight?"

Well, the truth was I wanted to rest up. See, I'd been playing behind Don Perkins so just about all my playing that year consisted of running up and down the field covering kicks. But we'd clinched the division the week before and I figured Landry ain't gonna take a chance of hurting Perkins in a meaningless game and I'd get my shot to show what I could do.

So I told Meredith, "Oh, I think I'll get some room service, watch a little TV and get to bed early."

"No, you're not," Meredith ordered. "Be down in the lobby in thirty minutes."

Now a rookie in those days did not question a veteran, especially not Meredith. See, Don was the team leader of the Cowboys on and off the field. You did what Meredith said.

So I got up, dressed and went downstairs. When I walked into the lobby Meredith was standing there wearing a chauffeur's cap. Somehow he'd wrangled a limousine for the night. So me and Meredith and Buddy Dial, Dan Reeves and Lee Roy Jordan take off in this stretch Lincoln. With Meredith at the wheel.

I didn't know it at the time but this was part of a tradition with the Cowboys. Sometime during the season on a road trip they would get each rookie drunk the night before a game. Rookies never played anyway so hangovers didn't mean a thing. There were only five rookies that year and tonight was my turn.

We get in the limo and Meredith turns around to me and says, "What do you want to drink tonight?"

"Oh, iced tea or something," I said.

"No," Meredith shot back, "I mean what do you want to *drink*?"

Oh, shit!

"Bourbon and seven?" I said.

"OK. You drink a drink every time I drink and I'm paying for it," Meredith says.

When we got to the restaurant Meredith tells the waiter, "Bring him a Crown Royale Mist."

Well, a Crown Royale Mist is nothing but a bourbon Sno-Kone. They take crushed ice and pour bourbon over it. It's worse than drinking straight out of the bottle because the ice takes away the bite so you can drink more.

I drink two or three and then I figured I better try to slow down this runaway train. Meredith is throwing down Scotch like it's lemonade and there's no way I can keep up with him. So I pour my next drink in a potted plant. And damned if Meredith don't catch me. He just looked at me real mean and said, "Don't ever do that again."

I don't know what time we got in or how many of those whiskey slushes I had but when I got up the next morning the last thing I wanted to do was play football. Finally I stumbled down to breakfast and Meredith looks like he just slept for forty-eight hours. He's bouncing around. He's singing and humming. He's laughing and telling jokes and I'm just barely managing to keep my eggs down.

We played the Steelers that afternoon and the whole goddamn game I don't get to play except on the suicide squads. It's the fourth quarter and Perkins is still out there. Meredith is still out there. What the hell is Landry thinking about? He's forgotten I'm there. It's a completely meaning-less game and I'm still on the bench.

Finally, with about two minutes left in the game, we got the ball and Landry looks around and says, "Hey, you, get in there." I don't think Landry knew my name the first three years I was with Dallas. It was always, "Hey, you!" So he points to me and I run on out there.

I get to the huddle and we're winning the game 37–6 and Meredith looks over to me and says, "Hey, Walt, how's it going?"

He knows exactly how it's going. I'm all hungover. My head's killing me. I've been covering kickoffs the whole game and my head's ringing inside that helmet like a Chinese gong.

"Well," Meredith says, "I've been reading all your clip-pings. You were some hotshot in college. Let's see what you got."

So he calls a "31 trap" which is right up the middle. The guard pulls, traps the nose tackle and you go right over the center whether there's a hole there or not. And no matter how many yards you make you're gonna take a beating— especially against Pittsburgh. Pittsburgh wasn't diddly then. You could always beat Pittsburgh but they would stomp the shit outta you along the way. They knew they couldn't beat you but they were gonna make you pay.

I carry the ball and make about a yard. And when I get back to the huddle Meredith says, "That ain't gonna do it. You were All-American. Let's try that again."

So he calls the same play right up the middle and this time I make 8 or 9 yards and just barely get the first down. "Now that's better," he says. "Let's run it again."

Same goddamn play! And I ran that damn thing nine straight downs until we ran the clock out. But along about the fourth play I snuck through a big hole in the line and two Pittsburgh linebackers made a sandwich outta me. One hit me high and the other tore my leg off. I got up sorta slow, but waved over to the sidelines that I was OK. I wanted to play so I limped back to the huddle and there's Meredith looking at me like I just tracked dogshit in on his new carpet.

"Let me tell you something," he says. "You ain't nothin but a little pussy. You're hurtin? Shit! You're nothin but a little pussy but I can't call you that in public so from now on I'm gonna call you "Little Puddin." But that means "Little Pussy." So every time I call you that you'll know what I'm talkin about."

And the name stuck. Little Puddin. Damn! I always wanted a nickname like Rocky or Bonecrusher or Jackhammer. But Little Puddin was my name. I go back to a Cowboy reunion even today and guys still call me that. "Hey, Puddin, what's happening?"

It was also Meredith who said the one line that people always quote when they're describing my football career. Once on *Monday Night Football* Meredith was talking about a running back and he said, "This guy reminds me a lot of Walt Garrison when he played. If you needed four yards, you'd give the ball to Walt and he'd get you four yards. If you needed twenty yards, you'd give the ball to Walt and he'd get you four yards."

Meredith was a brilliant guy. He not only knew the offense inside and out, he knew what every player did on every play. Meredith embarrassed me one day. We were going to a preseason game against the Rams so we drove from Thousand Oaks to the L.A. Coliseum in a bus. Meredith and I were sitting together talking about the game and Joe Don looked over at me and said, "How many audibles do we have from a red formation?"

"Do what?"

"What are the audibles for a switch against a Frisco Stack defense?"

"What language you speakin, kimosabe?"

"How many plays we got from brown and green formations?"

"I don't know."

"Well, you should know," he said. "Why should I have to tell you? When I call an audible at the line I'm telling you and you oughta know."

In fact, there was only one guy on the Cowboys who was smart enough to test wits or football smarts with Meredith—Dan Reeves, who's now the coach of the Denver Broncos. He'd give Meredith all sorts of crap.

Meredith was one of the best athletes on the Cowboys. But from the knees down Don was a wimp. His calves were like skinny old sticks of wood. In fact, he used to strap shin guards on under his socks to make his legs look bigger. But Reeves never let him forget he had those toothpicks down there. He always used to tell Meredith, "You should sue your legs for nonsupport."

Reeves was so knowledgeable he actually corrected Meredith at the line of scrimmage once. In a play-off game against Green Bay, Meredith called an audible that was the wrong play against the defense the Packers were running. And Reeves spotted the mistake in an instant.

Meredith gets up behind the center, looks around and yells out, "Red 3–67 . . ." And Reeves says sort of under his breath, "Sixty-eight! Sixty-eight!" And Meredith looks up over the line of scrimmage at the defense again and says, "Oh, ya. Red 3–68. . . ."

Nobody would have dared to correct Meredith like that—except Reeves, of course.

Dallas had a very complicated offense. Motion and divide—the famous Landry "multiple offense." On a pass route, for example, if you were a weak-side back, you'd run a circle. If you were a strong-side back, you'd run a straight route. The strong side was where the wingback lined up but if he went in motion then that was suddenly the weak side. If you're a little confused, I don't blame you because I know I sure was.

Donny Anderson was a rookie with the Packers when I was a rookie with the Cowboys. We'd played in the College All-Star game together and we were friends. So we were talking one time before a game and Donny said, "Hell, this is just like playing at Texas Tech—cut-and-dried offense." Lombardi ran a straight-ahead offense. Green Bay would sweep to the right, then sweep left. Then, on third down, they'd pass.

I told him about Landry's system and he said, "Holy shit, Walt! How do you learn all that stuff?"

"I don't, Donny, I don't."

Landry's offense could make a rookie look like a baboon with a reading disorder. Now as a veteran coming to camp you know the playbook from years past. They might change a few things here and there. But you've got it down cold in a week. But the rookies have got to learn not only the entire playbook, they've got to figure it out too. And none of it makes much sense.

So I started to study with Reeves and he made me a much better football player. Reeves is a very smart guy. It ain't an accident that he's taken the Denver Broncos to the last two Super Bowls.

He entered the University of South Carolina when he was sixteen and when he was a seventeen-year-old sopho-more, he was the starting quarterback for the Gamecocks. By the time he was through, he had broken all the school passing records. In his senior year he passed for 348 yards against Nebraska.

When he was twenty, Dan Reeves was the starting half-back for the Dallas Cowboys and just after he turned twenty-six, Landry named him a coach. At twenty-six! You think maybe the guy had some brains?

When Reeves showed up at Dallas they knew he wasn't going to make it as a quarterback. Not on a team that had Don Meredith, Craig Morton and Jerry Rhome. So they tried him at defensive back. And he wasn't really fast enough as a defensive back. So they tried him at receiver and he wasn't worth a shit there.

So they said, "Well, goddamn. This guy's doing a lot of things right. We gotta find a place for him." So they moved him to running back and he did a great job.

Frog had a phenomenal memory. He could remember everything about a game we played years before. He could remember every play, every drive, the number of plays in each drive, where we were on the field. That was his edge.

The problem was he'd go to a movie that lasted two hours and it'd take him three hours to describe it. His mind was like a projection booth. He drove us crazy. Frog went to Vietnam with a group of guys to visit the soldiers over there. It was a two-day trip and it took him two years to tell us about it. We heard about that damn trip every time we got together.

Somebody would mention Vietnam and Frog would say, "Vietnam. Did I tell you about the time Tommy Nobis was shootin this guy's machine gun. . . ."

His wife threatened to divorce him if he ever mentioned Vietnam again and he finally quit talking about it.

He had to be smart because Frog just wasn't all that talented. Hell, I could outrun Reeves. He won't agree with that but I could. It'd been a hell of a race to see who was the slowest running back in the NFL.

But Dan had more guts than a sumo wrestler and he loved to win. I am a fanatic about winning but Reeves makes me look like a wimp. Out in training camp somebody beat him at darts one night in a bar. He went out the next morning and bought a dart board. I didn't get any sleep for about a week because he's up all night—*fffunk, fffunk, fffunk, fffunk.* Throwing those darts. He went back the next week and kicked their ass.

Reeves taught me more about football than any coach I ever had. He played only six years but the guy was unbelievable. At night we'd go back to the room and he'd say, "Here's what you need to know, Walt. Now, do you understand the line blocking?"

"What the hell do I have to know the linemen's assignments for?" I'd want to know.

"Because if you know when they're blocking, you'll know the defenses."

"Why?"

"Because that makes a difference in how they're blocking. Then you need to know the secondary coverage. Like a '31 zone' from a '31 kick.' "

"I don't even know what a '31' is."

But Reeves wasn't just smart about football. He knew a sucker when he saw one—me.

When I was a rookie Reeves was a hot commodity around Dallas. People wanted him to speak at banquets and shopping centers all the time. So he called me one time.

"Hey, Walt, you want to do me a favor?"

"Sure, Frog, what is it?"

"I got two banquets to do tonight and I can't do them both. I'll let you do one of them if you want to and they'll pay you fifty dollars."

"God dang, Reeves," I said, "what do I have to do?"

"Just get up and tell a couple of jokes and I've got a highlight film for you. You can show it and then answer a few questions."

"Do I get to eat there?"

"Oh, ya," he said, "they'll feed you good."

"You mean all you want me to do is tell a couple jokes, show the film, answer some questions and they're gonna feed me *and* give me fifty dollars?"

"That's the deal."

"Boy," I said, "any of them you get that you don't want, you let me have em, Frog. Hell, I'll do one of them suckers every night."

See, when you're a rookie you get all the crappy deals. All the freebies and charity events. If they need a speaker for a YMCA or a Pop Warner team or the Rotary Club, you're it. So fifty bucks was a hell of a lot of money to me in those days and a free meal to boot. Hey, this was the high life of a football player I'd been hearing about.

So I did a couple of them and Meredith heard about it and he came up to me and said, "Why, you big dummy, you should charge at least a hundred fifty dollars. Reeves gets seven hundred fifty."

Seven hundred fifty dollars! I couldn't believe anybody would pay that much to hear a couple jokes and see some dumb-ass film. But if Reeves was getting $750 I wanted to know what Meredith was getting because Joe Don was the real celebrity on the Cowboys back in those days.

"Oh, I charge three thousand."

"My God! You're kidding, Don!"

"Ya. See, I don't like to make speeches but if they want to pay me three grand I love to do them."

"But, Joe Don," I said, "if I charge a hundred fifty, I won't get half as many of em."

"You dummy, you wouldn't need as many of them."

"Ya, that's right," I mumbled. See, Meredith wasn't just a better football player than I was, he was a better mathematician too.

Then I realized Reeves wasn't doing me a favor like I thought. He was just sticking me with the rinky-dink appearances that didn't pay enough.

"Hey, Puddin," Meredith said, "when are you gonna start using your head?"

He had me there. But how the hell was I supposed to know. Hey, I was just a dumb rookie.

CHAPTER TWO

LEWISVILLE, TEXAS, USA

It took me a long time to get that dumb. By the time I got
to the Cowboys, I was a full-bred country hick from Texas.
And damn proud of it too.

My daddy used to say, "If a guy's from Texas, he'll tell
you. If he ain't, for God's sake, don't bring it up and embar-
rass him."

I was born and raised in Lewisville, Texas. Well, actually I was born in Denton about twenty miles away because
Denton was the closest town to Lewisville that had a hospital.

Back in those days Lewisville had less than two thousand people, mostly farmers. On Main Street there was a
blacksmith shop and across from that the feed store and a
mule barn. Next to the mule barn was the Lewisville Hotel.
People used to say the Lewisville Hotel was like a tight pair
of Wrangler's—no ballroom. Fred Duwe bought the Dream-
land Theater and made a chute outta it to load his cattle and
Babe Frudy lived in a fixed-up streetcar. That's the kind of
town it was.

I'm glad I grew up in Lewisville. I think small towns give you something big towns don't. It's a slower pace. You have time to enjoy life more. In New York or Chicago or Dallas, it's go, go, go. Gotta do this. Gotta go here. In a small town it's, "Well, whadda ya wanna do today?"

"Well, I dunno. Go fishing? Shoot some pool? Wanna go downtown and listen to the ol guys bullshit?"

Ya, listening to the old farts bullshit was a big time in Lewisville. There used to be a whittlin bench next to the theater and I loved to come down there just to listen to an old guy named George Talley laugh. You could hear that guy laugh six blocks away. You could have heard him even farther away than that but that's all the blocks we had in Lewisville.

Then there was Tommie Nations, our scout master and volunteer fire chief. Only had one eye. The other one got put out by a BB. Tommie ran the blacksmith shop and wrote the society column for the Lewisville paper. You know, what's happening in Lewisville. Called the column "Hello, Nice People."

Used to be a bunch of trees over by the lumberyard and the old-timers would play dominoes when the weather was decent. In the morning they'd whittle in the shade of the building. Then when the sun would turn around in the afternoon, they'd come on over to the other side of Main Street and whittle over there.

On Saturday they'd show a movie over at the Liberty Theater. It was never at a set time or anything. An old guy named Henry Fletcher would stand out on the sidewalk in front of the theater and ring a triangle. Then everybody knew it was time for the movie to start and they'd come on down. Henry'd load everybody up with popcorn and soda and then he'd go upstairs and start the movie.

When I was five or so, the Liberty closed down and a while later a fellow built a new theater across the street. Andy Sisk was his name and the theater was called "The Andy." Hell of an inventive name, I thought.

So the movies was about it for entertainment in Lewisville. Oh, except for "Skate Night." We'd go roller skating on Saturday evenings at the Community Hall. That's where we had graduations or any big doins because we didn't have a gym at the high school. We'd even play basketball games there. It was kinda cramped. You'd make a lay-up and you'd hit the stage at one end and a brick wall at the other. They tore it down about twenty years back and built a post office in town. And even *that* was a big deal in Lewisville.

Now don't go gettin the impression that nothin ever happened in Lewisville. Hey, we had our share of excitement. In the late fifties one of the fellas who worked at the local insurance company killed himself after he got caught embezzling. He shot himself sitting in his car out by the water-tower. Poor old guy was keeping another lady besides his wife and that can get expensive. He was doing a little "travelin" (that's what they used to call it back in those days) and he needed some travelin expenses.

Another time when my mother was a little girl of nine or ten, she saw Bonnie and Clyde. She was standing on the side of the road and they drove by in one of those old-time touring cars with the low-cut doors so you could see right into the car. And on their laps were tommy guns. They just kinda waved and kept on going. But poor Momma was frozen there for about a half hour. She thought she was dead, sure. Course, she gets a big chuckle outta it today. What the hell they'd want to shoot up a nine-year-old girl for, only a nine-year-old girl could tell you.

Weird thing about it was Mother was one of the last humans ever to see Bonnie and Clyde alive 'cause the next day they shot em up like Swiss cheese over in East Texas.

Mother stayed home and took care of her four kids most of her life but now that Daddy's gone, she's got herself a job. Mother works at the funeral parlor. She buries people. After Daddy died she was looking for something to do and some friends owned a funeral home in Lewisville.

My wife and I were driving down the road one day and we see a funeral procession so we pull over and the hearse pulls up alongside us and Mother's driving. She rolls down the window and waves and yells, "How ya doin, honey?"

"Fine, Momma. How'd it go today?"

"Oh, just great," she says. "Planted two and burned one."

I don't know how she does it. "Mother," I told her, "that would be so depressing."

"Well," she says, "I know most of the people who are dyin. So I gotta go to the funeral anyway. I might as well get paid."

William Lloyd Garrison. That was my dad. But everybody called him Mutt. See, Daddy had a brother two years younger and they called them Mutt and Jeff. If you remember your comics, Mutt was the tall one. Dad was tall all right—about 6′ 3″—but Jeff grew up and he got bigger than Mutt but they still called Mutt, Mutt. We got most of our mail addressed to Mutt Garrison. You ask the people around here what my father's name was they'd say Mutt. They didn't even know his real name.

My daddy's father was a farmer—a sharecropper. He rented land here in Lewisville and worked it. So my father grew up on a farm and his dream was to someday have his own farm. But it was a tough way to make a living and he ended up working as a machinist at General Dynamics for thirty-five years. Worked his ass off his whole life and never complained.

He was a good man. When he died Roger Staubach and Dan Reeves and Lee Roy Jordan and a bunch of my former teammates flew in to be at his funeral. This was years after I'd retired.

I ain't saying Daddy was a saint. He liked to cuss and go to the beer joint and drink too much beer. He was a tough-minded guy. A disciplinarian. He wasn't like me. I hug my kids every day. Daddy wasn't thataway. I know he loved us because everything he did was for us. But as far as huggin and kissin—nah.

But my father never missed one of my football games in high school or college. I would look up every once in a while at practice in high school and his old car would be parked alongside the road. He might watch ten minutes or an hour and then drive on.

He never said, "You gotta play football. You gotta do this." He didn't care what I did but whatever I did he was there to support me. When I got married and had my first son I asked my dad, "How much should you give a kid?"

"Well," he said, "the easiest thing is to do what I did."

"What's that?"

"Give em everything you got."

When I look back on it, that's exactly what he did.

When I was playing at Oklahoma State, Mother and Daddy still made every football game I ever played. They went to games in Lincoln, Nebraska, Lawrence, Kansas, and Boulder, Colorado. And they drove to every game because they sure didn't have the money to fly. It was great but it was also kinda sad because, for instance, we'd play in Lincoln and I wouldn't see them before the game. We'd play and then after the game I'd get to see them maybe ten or fifteen minutes and then I'd have to get on the plane and they'd drive the seven hundred miles back to Lewisville. Seven hundred miles!

As soon as my father would get off work on Friday night they'd take off. Mother'd drive all Friday night and Saturday morning to get to the game. Then they'd turn around Saturday night and drive home.

Most of the way I am today is because I grew up in a small town in Texas. When I was a kid there wasn't a door locked in our house. Or anybody else's house. You never would have thought of anyone breaking into your house and stealing anything. If somebody needed something, they'd borrow it, even if you were gone. They'd just bring it back later and say, "I borrowed this while you were away and I'm bringing it back." And you were happy you could do something for a friend.

You just left things out in the open. You didn't try to hide anything because people never tried to steal it. Course, you didn't have much to steal. But you weren't used to much, so you were pretty well satisfied with what you had.

When we moved into our house my parents put down 50 dollars for the place, paid the deposit for lights and water and gas. (There wasn't any phone.) Then they went down and bought a bill of groceries. When they got home my daddy emptied his pockets and he had 47 cents left. But they never felt poor. Hell, they had something left and Daddy was working and he'd get paid again on Friday. So they weren't really worried about it. Hell, most people lived like that— paycheck to paycheck to paycheck.

I never went hungry. I always had clothes to wear. I didn't get to go to the movies or the skating rink on Saturday all the time. But kids were more inventive then about having fun so we never felt deprived. Heck, we roped calves. We slid down the hill on a piece of cardboard. We even had a bucking barrel in our backyard. It was the original mechanical bull. We'd get a big fifty-gallon barrel and hang it to a tree with four ropes and we'd put a bull rigging on it. You'd get up on that bull and try to hang on while a kid on each of the ropes was yanking and pulling and if you didn't hang on tight, they could throw you ten feet in the air.

In fact, most of what we did as kids revolved around horses and cattle. I was a cowboy long before I was a Cowboy. I grew up riding horses. When you're a country boy that's the way you're brought up. Horses and cattle and rodeoin are just a part of your life. In fact, my first job when I was about five or six was riding a horse. A lady here in Lewisville named Tom Jane Nowlin used to come by and get me. She had a horse that was crippled. It had fallen and broken its shoulder. Tom Jane was too heavy to ride him and I didn't weigh fifty pounds, so she'd come by the house with her horses and I'd get on the crippled one and we'd go riding in the country.

On Sundays Daddy used to take me out to Bud Ledbetter's dairy to ride the calves. He'd catch one and put one of us kids up on it and you'd try your best to get yourself killed. The big fun was to get bucked off and land on your head.

When I was about twelve, I entered my first rodeo, the Weatherford FFA Rodeo. For you city slickers, FFA means Future Farmers of America. There were five or six hundred kids entered in the rodeo and they had to rodeo all night long to get them all in. It was nothing but fun. I went to every rodeo I could after that.

My heroes in high school weren't Mickey Mantle or Johnny Unitas. They were all rodeo cowboys like Jack Buschbum, Jim Shoulders and Casey Tibbs.

I was playing a baseball game in high school once and me and a buddy of mine were supposed to go to a rodeo in Corsicana later that day. He comes up to me in the middle of the game and says, "Hey, man, we gotta go."

The game dragged on into extra innings and I had to go
tell the coach, "Coach Dieb, I gotta go."

"You gotta what?"

"I gotta go."

"What the hell for?"

"I got a rodeo."

"Well, get on outta here then." Hell, Coach Dieb loved
rodeoin too. Weren't no horses in baseball.

Tell you the truth, what I really wanted was to go to
college on a rodeo scholarship. I got offered one from Wharton Junior College. But my daddy talked me into going to
Oklahoma State because they were gonna give me a free ride
for four years to play football and the Wharton rodeo scholarship was only for two years. He said, "You're crazy to go
for two when you can get paid to go for four years."

So I ended up at OSU. But if one of the big four-year
rodeo schools like Texas Tech or Cal Poly San Luis Obispo
or Sam Houston had offered me a scholarship, I probably
would have gone there. And I woulda been content never to
play football cause in those days all I ever thought about was
rodeo. When I came home from college in the summer that's
all I'd do—rodeo. I never looked at a football.

Actually it was my father's garden that started me on
my way to football stardom. Daddy owned a half acre and
about half that was garden. But let me tell you, that black
dirt out here in Lewisville is tough to grow anything in. God
dang! You'd have to sit on a sack of fertilizer to raise an
umbrella. I hated that garden cause I was always in that
damn thing hoeing. But I found out that if I went out for
football, I didn't have to come home after school and work
in that damn garden. All of a sudden I loved football.

I played for the Lewisville High School Fightin Farmers. You think I'm kidding? If you drive by the watertower

here in town, you'll see a picture of a farmer with a pitchfork and a mean look. That's our mascot—the Fightin Farmer. You might think that's pretty funny but in Texas, high school football is serious business. You go to Wichita Falls High and they got a stadium there that's better'n most colleges got. Damn thing holds forty-five thousand. They've got a 30-second clock in both end zones and an electronic scoreboard right out of *Star Wars.*

During football season Lewisville would completely shut down for a football game. The stores all closed. Everybody just put a sign on their door "Gone to the game." By the time I got to high school there were about two thousand folks in Lewisville and you were liable to see all two thousand at the game.

My sister made the mistake of getting married on a Friday night when there was a game. She and my brother-in-law were at the altar, they were pronounced man and wife, they walked out the door and everybody followed them. And just kept right on going. They didn't even stay long enough to throw rice. The reception was at the football game. And my sister and her husband were there.

The thing I remember most about my high school football career was that we got beat a lot. We never had a winning season. If we won the coin flip before the game, we'd cut up. Damndest part of it was we had a good coach, Kent Clark. He's my insurance salesman now. The year after I graduated Coach Clark left Lewisville and went up to Lake Dallas, a little town around here, and kicked ass. So it musta been the players.

If you talk to the folks in Lewisville today who saw me play in high school, they'll all tell you what a great running back I was. "Oh, he ran wild." Even today I'll go back to some of the games to watch my son play and guys'll come up to me and say, "Oh, ya, we remember when you played.

You were great!" It's nice to be remembered. Only problem is they don't know what they're talking about.

At my best I was a mediocre high school football player. And I wasn't even a running back. I was a tackle for a while, then I was a linebacker. The only time I got to play running back in high school was when we played Northwest High in my senior year. They were the only team worse than we were. The score got to be 100-something to 6 and everybody on the team got to play whatever position they wanted in the second half. "Hey, Coach, let me go in and play quarterback."

"OK, get in there." So I got to run the ball a little that night.

Believe me, I never had the idea I was some hotshot football player because everybody in high school was better than I was. The hero of our high school team was Sammy Joe Sigler. He was phenomenal. He turned down scholarships to colleges everywhere and went to some little junior college and played a year or two and nobody ever heard of him again.

I wasn't a bad athlete. I held the pole vault record around these parts for a while at 10′ 6″. I didn't have a lot of technique though. If I wanted to go higher, I'd just take a longer run at it. I was also All-District in baseball. I was a catcher but I couldn't hit. If I'd come up with the bases loaded, they'd want me to bunt.

I ended up lettering in four sports in high school— football, basketball, baseball and track. Of course, when there's only a hundred kids in the whole school including girls, it ain't that hard to get a letter. It took every available body just to field a team, especially football. I still got a picture of my high school basketball team—all six of us including the coach. If you needed a rest during the game, you'd just kinda stand over to the side and let them run up and down the court a couple of times without you.

Besides lettering in four sports I was also elected "Most Handsome" in my senior class. Of course, there were only twenty-seven of us in the graduating class so it wasn't exactly like getting picked Mr. Universe. But I was still pretty puffed up about it cause my universe was Lewisville, Texas.

But like I was saying, I was no star in high school. If you'd seen me play and somebody had told you that someday that kid's going to play for the Dallas Cowboys, that would have got a pretty good laugh around town. In fact, after I got a scholarship to Oklahoma State one of my coaches said, "They musta been pretty hard up." My own coach.

People always wondered why I went off to Oklahoma to go to school. Why didn't you stay home in Texas? They could understand if I'd gone off to play for USC or Ohio State or maybe Hawaii or something. But Oklahoma State? Well, the truth is Oklahoma State was the only one who offered me a football scholarship. So when you only got one to choose from, it don't take you long to make up your mind.

When I was playing for Dallas, I asked Darrel Royal, the coach of the Texas Longhorns, why he didn't recruit me and he said, "Well, Walt, we took a look at you and you weren't any good."

For a long time I never knew the real reason Oklahoma State offered me that free ride. My daddy kept it from me cause I guess he didn't want to disillusion me. I figured when Oklahoma State asked me to play for them it was because I was some hotshot football star. But that wasn't exactly the way it was.

See, I used to work at the peanut mill down here in Lewisville—The American Nut Company—unloading boxcars of peanuts. I'd work the night shift from midnight to eight A.M. every Friday and Saturday night. On Friday night everybody would be going to the dance after the game so I'd kinda hang out at the dance for a while, then I'd go to work.

Well, Zan Burris who owned the nut factory had a brother John who was governor of New Mexico. Now Zan and my daddy were good friends so Zan said, "Let me call my brother and see if we can get Walt into some school somewhere." So he talked to his brother and the governor called all over and finally he pulled some strings with some bigshot in Oklahoma and they found a place for me at Oklahoma State.

So, see, the only reason I got even that one offer of a scholarship was not because of my football prowess but because I worked the graveyard shift at the American Nut Company.

I never had a car until my senior year in college because we could never afford one. So when I went to Oklahoma State up in Stillwater, Oklahoma, that was a big move for me. All two hundred fifty miles. But I'd never been nowhere so even going to Dallas twenty-five miles away was like the other end of the world for me.

My parents drove me up to OSU, checked me into my room in the dorm, put my stuff in the room, got in the car and left. The last thing my daddy told me was, "If you're not good enough and they don't want you up here, then come on home. But if you quit, just keep on going north, cause you ain't comin back."

So I had nowhere to go. I had to stay.

I tell you I was lost as an Easter egg when I first got there. I didn't know anybody. I was supposed to be rooming with another football player but he didn't show up so I was in a room by myself. Didn't know a soul.

I wandered around campus with nowhere to go. Stillwater's just a little bitty college town surrounded by ranches and farms. About the only thing to do in Stillwater is to drink. Lewisville is dry. Always has been. If you wanted to buy a beer, you'd have to go on over to Grapevine. So in Oklahoma my alcoholic little soul was in heaven. I was still underage, of course, but in Oklahoma you can drink at any age. If you got a buck and a quarter, you can drink in Oklahoma. It's almost a law. If you can buy it, you can drink it.

Milly's Bar and Grill was the local hangout in Stillwater. Old George ran this dumpy old place. The kind of place with dead flies on the windowsill and sawdust on the floor so you can spit. He named the joint after his wife Milly. What a tribute.

But I loved the place mostly because George would run you a tab. Up to 15 dollars. He knew if you were an athlete that's all the laundry money you got from the school. And he knew exactly when payday was and you better be there on that day to pay your tab or old George was on you like a bear in heat.

I was just a little bit green when I showed up at OSU. I didn't even know how to tie a tie. But we had to wear one on road trips to away games at OSU so my daddy had to tie me a tie. When I came in and took off my tie at night, I'd loosen the knot real carefully and pull it over my head and hang it up in the closet still tied. If it ever came untied, I was screwed.

Sammy Baugh was the freshman coach at OSU. Slingin Sammy from Rotan, Texas. Every fall he'd come up from Rotan and coach the freshman team, then head on back to his ranch when the season was over. Sammy's got six sections down in Rotan. Six hundred forty acres to a section. The whole thing's about six square miles.

Sammy was a hell of a football player in his day and he could still throw that football nine miles. And kick! Man, could he kick. He still holds a lot of NFL punting records. You'd run a pass pattern in practice and he'd punt the damn thing to you—this perfect spiral right to you, better'n our quarterback could *throw* it. You talk about punting the ball out of bounds where you wanted to. Sammy could land that mother on a politician's heart.

I loved Sammy. He was a down-home boy. He'd come to practice in boots, blue jeans, a T-shirt and a baseball cap. Once I asked Sammy what he wanted us to wear to away games. "Suit and tie, Coach?"

"I don't give a damn if you show up nekkid, as long as you come ready to play."

Sammy's game-day attire was one of those red and black flannel hunting shirts with a little string tie and a cowboy hat.

Playing for Sammy was nothing but fun. But the next year when I joined the varsity it was a whole nother story.

Cliff Spiegel, who was the head coach at OSU, got fired after my freshman year and they hired a guy named Phil Cutchin. Phil was an assistant under Bear Bryant at Alabama and coached in the NFL awhile. He was a tough sonuvabitch. Cutchin came in and laid down a bunch of rules and you followed em baby or your butt was gone. Under Cutchin you not only had to work like a mule on the field, you had to do things like write your mother once a week and keep your room clean and be at study hall every night. One of the assistant coaches ran the study hall and you came and studied and if you didn't, you were in Cutchin's office the next day explaining why. Cutchin told us, "You gotta have good work habits, in school and on the football field, if you wanna succeed."

Cutchin also had a ten o'clock curfew and nobody, I mean *nobody* ever broke it. That's how scared we were of Cutchin.

Cutchin was tough. One hundred twenty came out for spring football. Three weeks later, there were twenty-seven of us left! He ran everybody off. "There's a lot of people up here who don't wanna play football who are using up our scholarships," he told us. "If you wanna play, we got a place for you. If you don't wanna play, we ain't got a place for you."

One of my teammates that spring was a big black guy named Jerome Bell. He was a specimen. Big and strong. He could run 9.5 and punt the ball eight miles. But he upped and quit one day. And once you quit with Coach Cutchin that was the end.

Jerome thought it over and the next day he came back and pleaded with Cutchin to let him back on the team. Then Jerome's mother called and said football was the only way Jerome could go to school and stuff like that. So the next day Coach Cutchin gathered the team together and said, "Jerome here quit but he wants to come back. I'm going to leave it up to you. But, remember, he's quit you once and he may quit you again when you need him the most."

Well, everybody voted for him to stay including me— and it didn't take us long to make up our minds either. We weren't no dummies. Jerome was a hell of an athlete. Six-four and faster than an antelope's fart. Hell, at Oklahoma State we just didn't get many players like Jerome Bell. The roster at OSU was filled with guys like Walt Garrison who made their names not on the gridiron but at the loading dock at some nut factory. So we all voted for Jerome to stay.

Cutchin said, "All right, but I'll tell you one thing. I guarantee you he won't quit you again because every day after practice while you're all in there gettin your shower and dressin, we're gonna run Jerome here to death."

And Cutchin is going on and on about how he was gonna work poor Jerome to an inch of his life and Jerome's eyes are getting bigger and bigger and this look of horror comes over his face and the next thing we know, there goes Jerome heading out the gate. The last time I ever saw Jerome Bell he was using that 9.5 speed of his to get as far away from Phil Cutchin as he possibly could.

In the end, Cutchin turned out to be a nice guy. Once the season was over in your senior year, he was great. He'd invite you over to his house to have a beer or a barbecue. He was just a good guy. But before that he was a miserable sonuvabitch.

Coach Cutchin is the guy who changed me from a line-backer to a running back. I couldn't tell you why he did it. The guy who was playing fullback for OSU at the time was named Hugh McCrabb. He was an All-State back from Oklahoma. He was tough and fast and he won every award there was in high school. Cutchin made him a nose guard. It damn near killed him.

Then we had a guy name of George Thomas who was also a fullback. He was a year ahead of me and we split time for about five games. Then Cutchin moved George to defensive end.

I don't know why and I still don't. Because I swear both those guys, McCrabb and Thomas, could run circles around me. It never made any sense to me but, without a doubt, it was the greatest thing that ever happened to me.

My whole career was a series of lucky breaks. I got that gift scholarship to OSU, then Cutchin changes me to fullback. I never could have made it to the pros at any other position. I wasn't fast enough to be a defensive back and I was too small for linebacker. It turned out great for me. My junior year I led the Big Eight in rushing and was second-team All-Big Eight behind Oklahoma's Jim Grisham. Then I made first-team All Big Eight my senior year and came in second in the rushing title, 5 yards behind Charley Brown from Missouri. I was also second-team All-American that year behind Jim Grabowski, the great back from Illinois.

Unfortunately, we didn't win a lot of games at OSU. Our schedule was filled with Big Eight teams like Nebraska, Oklahoma, Colorado and Iowa State. Besides that, we opened our season every year against Arkansas down in Fayetteville. And they used to just beat the daylights outta us.

I always thought, "Who is the masochist putting this schedule together? Let's schedule some easy teams. How about a couple junior colleges?" But we had no breathers at OSU. We never eased into the season. We were the soft touch that teams like Arkansas scheduled to ease into *their* season.

We did have our moments though. My sophomore year, 1964, we played Texas. That was the year they won the national championship. They were 35-point favorites. And we got hot early on them—which turned out to be a big mistake. They kicked a field goal on their first possession but on the next play I ran 50-something yards for a TD. We were the only team ever to be ahead of Texas that entire season. And all that did was piss em off. They just beat the hell out of us up and down the field the rest of the day. Oh, man, they had some horses—Tommy Nobis, Scott Appleton—a line whose weight averaged about 265 to 270. And they just whipped us like a bad puppy—38–7.

In my senior year we were 3–7 but in the last game of the season we beat Oklahoma University. OSU never beat Oklahoma. Ralph Neely was from OU and when we both played for the Cowboys he and I would bet a fifth of Scotch every year on the game. I lost a lot of booze to Neely over the years.

But we won in 1965. It's probably the greatest victory in Oklahoma State history. The 1965 team is famous for that win. OU was shooting for another national title for head coach Bud Wilkinson. But we kicked a last-second field goal and beat them 17–16. Stillwater lost its mind. They tore down the goal posts. They threw the coaches in the shower. They declared a school holiday and shut the whole town down— except for the bars, of course. You could walk into any bar in town and if you were a football player, everybody wanted to buy you a beer. It was big doins.

Probably the biggest thrill in college for me was the game we played at Nebraska my senior year. Nebraska was supposed to kill everybody that year and mostly they did. We were behind 17–7 in the last quarter and we scored to make it 17–14. We kicked off, held and got the ball back on our own 30 with a minute and a bit left on the clock. I carried the ball seven times in that drive and on the last play of the game I wound up on Nebraska's 2-yard line.

Bob Devaney, the Nebraska head coach, came out on the field and shook my hand, which was a big thrill for me. Of course, we still got beat so it kinda tarnished the tribute. I would have liked it a whole lot better if we'd won and Devaney woulda tried to come out there and kick me in the ass.

CHAPTER THREE

LOOK MA, I'M A COWBOY

I never had a clue that Dallas was going to draft me. I never thought about playing pro ball. It just never crossed my mind I'd be good enough to get a look. I gained a bunch of yards at OSU but we got killed about every game and, besides, we didn't have a passing attack, so they had to give me the ball. I was just tickled as hell to be getting a free education. Pro ball was the farthest thing from my mind.

In a player's senior year if a pro team is interested in him they send out these letters with a questionnaire enclosed— name, height, weight. That kind of stuff. I got one from the Cowboys and one from the Rams.

And I thought, "Gal dang. This is great."

Only thing was there was a guy from Midlands, Texas, named Jeff Edwards who was born with one leg shorter than the other. He was a hell of a football player but his leg and hip got to botherin him so after his sophomore year he had to quit and he became the equipment manager for the team. And you know what? He got the same goddamn letters I got. Only he got one from *three* teams.

That sorta burst my bubble.

The first inkling I had that a pro team was really serious about me happened a couple weeks before the draft when the Los Angeles Rams sent a "babysitter" out to Stillwater to watch over me. In those days the NFL and AFL had not yet merged so the two leagues were fighting for players. The big-name collegiate stars were getting unbelievable bucks to sign. The year I signed with the Cowboys, Donny Anderson and Jim Grabowski went to Green Bay in a million-dollar deal. Donny got $715,000 and Jim hauled in $400,000. They called them "The Golddust Twins."

In order to try to keep the contracts from spiraling out of sight, Pete Rozelle directed all the NFL clubs to send out babysitters to keep as many of their future draft picks as possible out of the clutches of the AFL scouts.

So one day this guy from the Rams shows up at my door. I didn't know who or what the hell he was but I loved his attitude.

"I'm from the Rams," he says. "I'm going to take you and your buddies out to eat."

It was great. We'd go out, eat like hogs on holiday, drink beer till we'd bust—and he's pickin up the bill. The guy even bought me a brand-new pair of boots.

"You want some new boots, Walt?"

"You're goddamn right I'll take some boots!" I wasn't proud. I was still busted. Didn't have a dollar on the good days.

He kept telling me, "The Rams are going to draft you in the sixth round." And then he'd buy me and my friends another beer. I thought Sanny Claus had picked up and moved to Oklahoma. Only problem was when draft day came the Cowboys drafted me in the *fifth* round and Sanny Claus left town pissed off.

And that's when Gil Brandt slithered into my life.

· · ·

Gil Brandt was the Dallas Cowboys' director of personnel. In other words, the head scout. He'd find the best collegiate prospects and try and sign them.

Before he worked for the Cowboys, Brandt was a baby photographer. He'd teach the nurses in the maternity wards around town how to take pictures of the newborn babies and they'd get a slice of the action.

As a hobby, Brandt would rate college players as pro prospects and send his findings to the Rams where Tex Schramm was the general manager at the time. And damned if most of his picks didn't pan out. After a couple years Tex said, "Hey, this guy's pretty good." So when Tex took over as general manager at Dallas, he hired Gil.

Brandt was good at what he did. Everybody knows Cliff Harris and Drew Pearson and Rayfield Wright and Cornell Green. But nobody had ever heard of those guys in college. Hell, Cornell Green never even played a game of college football. He was a basketball player at Utah State and he turned out to be All-Pro at two positions! Jethro Pugh was from Elizabeth City College and Rayfield went to Fort Valley State. Take my word for it, those are actual colleges. Cliff Harris was from Ouachita Baptist, for Christ's sake. Pete Gent was another basketball player who never played collegiate football and Drew Pearson was a free agent from Tulsa who everybody else passed on.

Gil Brandt discovered all those guys. He drafted Calvin Hill out of Yale and everybody said what a stupid move it was. "There ain't nobody from Yale that can play in the NFL." Calvin was Rookie of the Year.

Now today a lot of pros come out of small colleges you never heard of. But back in the sixties, Brandt was the only one really mining those little-known schools for talent.

Brandt was good for the Cowboys and he was a hell of a negotiator. A rookie trying to cut a deal with Gil was like a calf being trucked to the slaughterhouse.

Brandt liked to sign a rookie to a so-called "three-year contract" which in reality was a series of three one-year contracts linked together by absolutely nothing except the imagination and ignorance of the dumb rookie.

When Cliff Harris signed with the Cowboys, Brandt told poor Cliff he was getting a special deal. Instead of a one-year or two-year contract, he was going to get a three-year contract. Well, of course, Cliff jumped at the chance to get himself in solid with the Cowboys. When he signed that contract he had them right where they wanted him.

He was a happy little camper and he went around asking all the rookies in training camp how many years they got. And they mostly all said, "One."

"How about you?"

"One."

"And you?"

"One."

And Cliff is gloating and he says, "Well, shit, I got a three-year contract."

"A three-year contract. Don't you know you're getting screwed?"

"Whadda ya mean?"

"Hell, you're stuck with the money they signed you to. If you make All-Pro or you start or you're Rookie of the Year, they still only have to pay you that piddly rookie money. But if you're a bust, they cut your ass and you don't get dime one."

"Oh, shit."

Poor Cliff was stuck for three years at minimum wage.

Another bit of tinsel that Gil liked to flash at rookies was his alligator shoes. He still owes me a pair. Whenever you're a rookie fixin to sign, Gil's real nice to you. Anything you want, you got. And he had a pair of alligator shoes with little tassels on them that just set my heart on fire.

I'd never had a pair of alligator shoes before and Gil says, "I'll get you a pair. No cost. You want brown? Black?"

"Well . . . brown."

"No problem. You got em."

That's the last I ever heard about those shoes and that was 1965.

Gil went up to Clemson to sign Charlie Waters one year and he's got on the alligator shoes. They had those same little tassels on them that sucked me in. Charlie admires the shoes and Gil says, "No problem. You got em."

Does this sound familiar? Well, Charlie and Gil dicker back and forth over the terms of Charlie's contract and they can't make a deal. So Gil leaves Clemson and three days later Charlie gets a brand-new pair of alligator shoes in the mail. And they were gorgeous. A perfect fit with those little tassels.

So, finally, with Charlie all softened up with his new shoes, they cut a deal the next day. And three days later in the mail, Charlie gets an invoice for $280 for those goddamn alligator shoes.

One year at training camp out in California, I was trying to get a golf shirt or something with a Dallas Cowboy logo on it for my aunt and uncle who were in town. I figured I'd get them a couple souvenir shirts, they'd go back to Texas and brag to all the folks. Give em a thrill. So I went over to my buddy Gil and said, "Gil, I need a couple of those Dallas Cowboy T-shirts."

"Oh, no way. We only give those out to the players. That's it. No exceptions."

So I felt like hell going back to my aunt and uncle and telling them I couldn't get them their shirts.

The next day I went down to some beer joint Gil used

to go to a lot and every waitress in the goddamn place had a Dallas Cowboy T-shirt on. I said, "Where did you get those T-shirts?"

"Oh, Mr. Brandt was down here. What a nice guy."

Ya, what a nice guy.

Gil was always trying something. We played the San Francisco 49ers one year and got in a big fight with them. Both benches cleared and there were fights all over the field. I ended up fighting with Ed Biggs. He was a bad *hombre*. I didn't really want to take him on but he was there and so I started swinging.

We ended up over by the sidelines and Gil tried to kick Biggs in the ass while we were in a big pile. He kinda crept up real sneaky like and got a boot in while Biggs was occupied with a few other matters—like about half a dozen Cowboys.

But Gil never figured on one little thing—the game films. As soon as Biggs saw those films and saw Gil over there takin a cheap shot at him, he let it be known all over the league that he was gonna get Brandt.

Now Gil always stood on the sidelines during the games. Always. He didn't do nothing but stand there looking like he was a big shot. Everyone in the stands thought he was a coach. All he did was get in the way. But the next time we played the 49ers, Gil was a scarce item. Biggs was looking for him and Gil knew it. On the plane ride home after the game we were all getting on Gil.

"Hey, Gil, where you been? We missed you."

All he could do was smile.

Thankfully, Gil Brandt didn't have anything to do with negotiating with you after your rookie year. He found the players and signed them. That was his job.

After that I negotiated my contracts with Al Ward, the

assistant general manager. It was just glorified horse tradin which I enjoyed. I liked saying, "Al, that ain't enough money and if you can't come up with a better offer than that, don't bother to call me."

Course then I'd start thinking, "Goddamn, I hope he calls me. What have I done?" But then that paranoia is part of the fun of horse tradin.

I actually flipped a coin over the phone for a thousand bucks one time with Al. I was at a rodeo somewhere and Al finally tracked me down and called me. We were a thousand bucks apart and I wouldn't budge and he wouldn't either. So he said, "Let's just flip a coin."

"Who's gonna flip the coin?" I asked.

"Walt," he said, "you're honest. You flip the coin. And I'll call it."

"Al, you're not gonna win. I'm gonna tell you whatever's opposite of what you call. A thousand bucks don't mean a thing to you because it don't come out of your pocket. But you're talking about my salary, my family, my kids."

"No, Walt, you wouldn't do that."

"All right, Al. Here goes." And I flipped the coin on the bed in the hotel room.

Al called "heads." And it was tails. And I said, "Al, it's tails."

"All right, you got it," he said.

I've often wondered what would've happened if it had landed heads. Who knows?

Actually, when I was talking to Al Ward I was really talking to Tex Schramm, the Cowboys' general manager. Al would say, "Excuse me, I've got to go to the bathroom." And he'd be back in an hour and a half and say, "Ya, OK, we'll give you that." And all he'd done was go and talk to Schramm and Tex'd say, "Ya, go ahead with the deal."

In fact, I always wanted to negotiate with Tex because

that's who Al was talking to anyway. One time I said to Al, "Why don't you let me go in there with Tex. I know that's where you're going anyway."

"No, I'm the one handling your contract," Al said. So that's how we did it. Seemed kinda dumb to me.

A lot of people didn't like Tex. But I always did. I still do. I think he's a great guy and I think he's done a great job for the Cowboys and the NFL. Tex is good for football. He's on the rules committee. He represents the owners in a lot of stuff. He's smart and they trust him. He's out for the good of the game. He was a big part of the NFL's experiment with the instant replay, for example.

But I also like Tex personally. He's a good guy. When they have the Cowboy reunions, Tex is the first one there. When you get there, he's there. And when you leave, he's still there. Now you're talking about the general manager. You're not talking about somebody whose turn it is to run the show that night. Nah, Tex just enjoys seeing the old players. And I like that. It says something about the man. He still treats you good, he still knows your name, even after you aren't helping the team anymore. A lot of people ain't that way.

Tex is smart. He stayed out of the day-to-day operations of the team. He left that up to Tom Landry. There's a lot of general managers who are all over the coach. "Why aren't you doing this? You gotta do that."

Tex would never come to practice and say, "Hey, Tom, here's a good play I drew up last night."

Tex did what a general manager is supposed to do. He managed the team in general. He got a guy to run the football team—Tom Landry. He got a guy to handle the scouting operation—Gil Brandt. He got a guy to handle the PR department—Doug Todd. Tex oversaw the overall operation and then he reported to one man—the owner, Clint Murchison.

. . .

Like I was saying it was a real shock to me when Dallas drafted me. Gil came up to watch our practice at OSU along with two or three other guys but I didn't know who he was at the time. I don't even know if they were looking at me. We had a couple of other pretty good players on the team. Charlie Harper, a tackle, was drafted by the Giants and Charlie Durkee, our kicker, was taken as a free agent by the Cowboys. So I don't know who they were looking at or why.

Draft day came and Dallas took me as their third choice overall and the next week Gil came up to Stillwater and we discussed contracts. And I tell you I didn't know what the hell he was talking about. Gil said he was gonna give me $15,000 a year and another $15,000 as a bonus for signing. Hell, my dad made $6,000 a year for working seven to four every day for thirty-five years.

When some guy comes up to you and you been poor your whole life and they say they're gonna put fifteen grand in your pocket, I tell you, it makes you wonder if those mushrooms you ate for lunch weren't doused with something.

"You're gonna give me fifteen thousand dollars *cash* to play football. Are you shittin me! When do I gotta give it back?"

Besides that, even though Kansas City of the AFL had drafted me in the nineteenth round, I was from Dallas. Hell, I woulda signed for lunch money. Thank God, Gil didn't know that.

Then Gil said, "We're gonna buy you a new car. Any kind you want." And I'm trying to act nonchalant because I'd been trying to get ready to negotiate with this fella for a few days now and he starts out about $10,000 higher than I thought I was worth. Kinda takes the wind outta your sails.

When I got my breath back I thought, "Ah, what the hell." So I said, "There's two other things I want."

"What's that?"

"I want you to fly my parents first class to the East-West Shrine Game to watch me play."

"OK."

"And I want a two-horse, in-line trailer."

"A what?" Players had asked the Cowboys for just about everything over the years but never a horse trailer.

"A two-horse, in-line trailer."

"What the hell is that?"

"It's a trailer where the horses are one behind the other."

So he says, "Wait a minute." And he goes down to the phone and calls Tex.

"Goddamn, Tex, this kid wants a two-horse, in-line trailer."

"Ya, what's it cost?"

"I don't know."

"Find out. And if it don't cost that much, get it for him."

Well, at that time, they cost about $2,200. The best one you could buy. So they got it for me. That and a brand-new green and white Pontiac Grand Prix to go with my green and white horse trailer. I used to drive my flashy new rig up and down Main Street.

It was a big deal in Lewisville when I joined the Cowboys. It's a football town in a football state. Now, I didn't actually think I could make it in the NFL but I wanted to be able to say I had played for the Dallas Cowboys. So my goal when I first signed was just to play one year on the taxi squad. If I could just stick it out for a season on the cab team, even though I wouldn't get to suit up for the games, I could come home to Lewisville and be a star. I could go down to the Dairy Queen which was the big hangout at the time and I'd be cool.

See, it was my life's ambition at the time to wow em at the Dairy Queen. After I signed with the Cowboys I started carrying a one-hundred-dollar bill. And I'd get about forty or fifty one-dollar bills and I'd put that hundred right on top. Just like the big boys. I had a wad I could barely fit in my back pocket. Looked like $10,000.

But I didn't stop there. I got to drinking Wild Turkey bourbon. That was cool with the Dairy Queen crowd too. I bought me a whole case of it and put it in the trunk of my new Grand Prix. When I was at the beer joint or the Dairy Queen, I'd say, "Hey, y'all wanna drink?"

So we'd go on out to my car and I'd raise the trunk and there'd be a whole goddamn case of Wild Turkey. I'd pull a bottle out and fix everybody a drink. *Oooo, weeee,* that was cool. But the next day I'd be sure and go down to the liquor store and buy another bottle to replace the one I just drank. So it looked like I was buyin a case of that stuff about every other day. But I could only afford that one case, so in order to impress everyone, I had to keep it full up.

And back in those days, impressing the folks in Lewisville was a top priority of mine because to me Lewisville, Texas, was my Big Apple.

PART TWO

☆ AMERICA'S TEAM

CHAPTER FOUR

THE MAN IN THE IRON FACE

The Dallas Cowboys were born in 1960 when the NFL, headed by Papa George Halas of the Chicago Bears, sold Clint Murchison an NFL franchise for $600,000. Born is probably too grand a word. It was more like hatched because in the beginning the Cowboys were a real turkey.

The Cowboys got most of their players in a special expansion draft in which Dallas got to choose three players from each of the other NFL teams. But first those teams were allowed to "freeze" the top twenty-five players on their rosters and the Cowboy brass got to pick from what was left.

What was left was slim pickins. Mostly a bunch of marginal players with little talent or good players on the downhill side of their careers, or guys with an attitude.

And the NFL gave Landry and his crew twenty-four hours to do their choosing. Gee thanks!

It was a real shaky deal those first few years. The team offices were in a room shared by an auto club. Practices were held at Burnett Field, an old baseball diamond. The players weren't the only ones using the lockers at this cockroach den. They'd come back from practice and find rats had eaten the tongues out of their shoes. When they'd shower, scorpions would scoot across the shower floor.

The early Cowboy teams were worse than bad. They didn't win a game the first year. In the twelfth game of the season, they managed a tie with the New York Giants, 31–31, and they tore the locker room apart celebrating.

The *NFL Bloopers* and *The Cowboys' Highlights* were the same film. They'd just put a different title on it and send it on out.

In 1962 in a game against the Steelers, Cowboy Eddie LaBaron threw a 99-yard TD bomb to Frank Clark. But Dallas guard Andy Cvercko was caught holding on the play in the end zone. According to the rules at that time, the other team was awarded a safety when you committed a foul in your own end zone. So the longest TD in Cowboys' history was wiped out and Pittsburgh got two points.

That's the way things went for the Cowboys in those days.

In 1961 Dallas beat Washington and it made their year. They were 4-9-1. In 1962 they won five games but in 1963 they had only one victory. In 1964 they were back up to five wins, eight losses and a tie.

But Landry was slowly building his team. He had Meredith at quarterback and Bob Lilly at defensive tackle but there just weren't enough good players to help those guys out.

Then things started to turn around for the Cowboys in 1965. That year's draft was one of the best in the club's history. First, they landed Craig Morton, a quarterback from California with a 45-caliber arm, who would eventually lead the Cowboys to two Super Bowls. Dallas also got Ralph Neely, an offensive tackle from Oklahoma, who was All-Pro for the next decade. And Bob Hayes, the fastest man in the solar system, and Jethro Pugh and Dan Reeves and Jerry Rhome.

Dallas promptly started to win some games. They ended up 7–7 in 1965, finished second in their division and got a trip to the Runner-up Bowl in Miami.

In 1966, 1967, 1968 and 1969, Dallas continued to draft quality players and the winning snowballed. My first year with the Cowboys, 1966, we were 10–3 and played Green Bay for the NFL championship. And the winning never stopped. The Cowboys went twenty-two straight years without a losing season.

It wasn't an accident that Dallas was so successful. The Cowboys had a plan and the chief architect of that plan was Tom Landry. We're talking about a very smart boy here, folks. This guy could have been just about anything he wanted because he had a ferocious will to win and brains leaking out his ears.

They throw the word genius around pretty loosely these days. But that's what Landry is. Most of us are copiers. And if you're a really smart guy, you figure out what the best things are and why they're the best and you use them. You copy.

Landry's a couple light years ahead of that. He's the kind of guy who invents the stuff that the rest of us copy. He looked at football the way it was being played at the time and he devised completely new systems on offense *and* defense to beat that game. And for the last twenty years, the rest of the league has been trying to understand and then copy what Landry invented.

That's called a genius.

Landry invented the Flex Defense out of thin air. He designed it. He developed it. He choreographed it. He did it all. When Tom was the young defensive coordinator for the Giants, they played a simple 4–3 defense. Then Tom's mind got churning and before long the Flex Defense was a reality.

The Flex Defense is simply an undershifted or overshifted defensive line. If you were flexed strong, you'd line up in a 4–3 but really you were going to play an overshifted defense. When you were flexed weak, you'd line up in a 4–3 but you were really playing an undershifted defense.

The advantage was that you could play a lot of different defenses and get it all to look the same to your opponent. The quarterback would get up to the line of scrimmage, see a 4–3 defense lined up in front of him, call an audible to beat it and, at the snap of the ball, everything suddenly changed.

Each player in the Flex had to learn to read "keys" from the action of the offensive players and then react with a move that Landry figured to be the most effective in that situation. The defense was dependent on players going to an assigned area and "holding." The theory being that if every man was in the proper place the offense went nowhere.

See, the Flex is a gap-control defense. The offensive theory back then was headed by Vince Lombardi's "run to daylight" offense. They'd give the ball to the running back and when he'd see a hole open, a little daylight, he'd break for it. He'd run to daylight.

Now, with the gap defense, the defensive man would plug up the holes and there wasn't any daylight to run to. The only problem is, it's a very disciplined system. If somebody doesn't do his job, the coordination of the whole thing will be broken and there will be daylight all over the place.

Players can lose confidence in it easily. You can see some gaping holes in the Flex because when your linemen fill up the gaps, you no longer have players lined up equally spaced out. There might be twenty feet between defensive linemen.

The key to the Flex was to have a bunch of good football players who didn't make mistakes. People who were disciplined enough to play their position and smart enough to know what they were supposed to do.

And that was gonna take some time and some talent.

Landry and Hank Stram of the Kansas City Chiefs are usually credited with the development of the Multiple-Set Offense. But nobody, including Kansas City, used the Multiple-Set with as much variation or as much success.

Landry developed his offense by looking at it from a defensive point of view. He noted what caused his own defense the most problems and went from there.

He had always felt that one of the easiest teams to defend against was a team that just sat there in one or two formations. What caused fits was a team that gave you a lot of different looks—different formations and lots of movement. An offense that constantly forced you to make adjustments even as the play was getting under way.

If you were gonna run just a basic set offense, you had to have great athletes. You had to have a team like the Green Bay Packers of the sixties. A huge line with a couple of Hall of Fame running backs behind it like Jim Taylor and Paul Hornung. Green Bay just said, "Here we come. Stop us if you can." And nobody could because their players were so great.

But in those early years at Dallas, great players were very few and very far between. Landry knew that the only way to move the ball with the talent he had was to outsmart everybody else. He felt that with the Multiple-Set offense he could move the football and score points with less talent. And, of course, if and when he came up with some really talented players, Dallas could run wild using the same concept. And that's exactly what happened.

In 1966 the Cowboys scored 445 points in only fourteen games, a record that held up until 1980 when they scored 454 points in a sixteen-game schedule and came back and scored 479 in 1983. That's puttin some points on the board!

Before Landry came along coaches used shifts and different formations but nobody did what Landry did. Nobody at that time was also shifting the line, blocking the view of the defense so they couldn't see what we were up to in the backfield. Every play was a surprise. After a while they didn't know what was coming at them. Confusion reigned like turds at a horse show.

It's hard enough to stop a good offense when you know what they're up to. But when you haven't got a clue what they're gonna do next, it's devastating. That was the trademark of the Dallas teams. They had no trademark. You could never say, "Oh, Dallas loves to pass or run." They did it all from every position and formation.

Again, the problem was you had to have players who could understand what the hell Landry was talking about. Meredith had a good line. "I took a page of Landry's playbook to a Chinese laundry and they gave me three shirts and a pillowcase."

The Cowboys used to give IQ tests to prospects and if they didn't score high enough, they wouldn't touch them. The Cowboys just didn't draft players unless their intelligence level was high. They always looked at physical skills but if a player didn't have it upstairs, he couldn't cut it at Dallas because you had a goddamn intellectual devising the game plan. It was like having Socrates as your coach. Year after year we had guys who came in with talent to burn but they couldn't make the team because they couldn't learn the system. The guy could run a 4.4 forty but if he couldn't understand the playbook, he wasn't gonna do Landry much good.

. . .

It took a few years before people began to believe the mumbo jumbo Landry was throwing around. Especially the players. Now if they'd known Landry was going to fashion the Cowboys into the winningest team in the NFL over the next twenty years, it woulda been a lot easier to swallow all this weird crap Landry was trying to force feed them. But when you lose 76 percent of your games the first four years like Landry did, it takes a farsighted individual to think you're anything but a crackpot with some dipshit ideas.

When he first took over as head coach, Landry had a bunch of old dogs who he'd gotten from the other NFL teams and he was trying to teach them all these new tricks. And they bitched like hell about it. "What the hell are you talkin about? Let's just play some goddamn football. Snap the damn ball and block and tackle."

They were all against Landry in the beginning. He lost like hell those first five years and, to tell the truth, he'd probably have been sent packing just about anywhere else.

But that's where Clint Murchison came in. Clint just happened to own the Cowboys. And he knew a genius when he saw one. After the fourth dismal year in a row, everybody in Dallas was looking for Landry's head. Why not? Tom's record was 13–38–3. Ouch!

Clint called a press conference and everybody thought, "Oh, boy. He's gonna get rid of the bum."

Instead, Clint signed Landry to a ten-year deal—the biggest contract in NFL history. "Well, that oughta quiet them down," Clint said.

That's smart business. He had the man he wanted and he was gonna keep him. And to hell with the press. Which is what he was saying. "Screw you guys. I'm running this team."

I really liked Clint. He wasn't like a lot of owners. He

put up the cash without trying to run the team. Clint stayed out of the way. I saw him at the practice field three or four times in nine years. He was just never around.

"I do not offer suggestions to Tom Landry," he said one time. "Furthermore, Landry never makes any suggestions as to how I conduct my sixth-grade football team, which, incidentally, is undefeated. We have a professional standoff."

The truth is everybody thought Clint was crazy to buy the Cowboys in the first place. But when you have the kind of dough he had, you can afford to be a little crazy.

The first year of operation the Cowboys cost Clint a cool million. So the sportswriters went to his daddy, Clint, Sr., and said, "What do you think about your boy losing a million dollars in his first year?"

And his old man said, "Well, at that pace he can only last another hundred forty-two more years."

His business critics shouldn't have been too concerned. Murchison bought the Cowboys for $600,000 and unloaded them in 1985 for something in the vicinity of eighty million.

Now that's not such a bad profit.

If people had a hard time figuring out Landry's system, it was nothing compared with the trouble they had trying to figure out his personality.

A reporter once asked me if I'd ever seen Tom Landry smile.

"No," I answered, "I only played nine years. But I know he smiled at least three times cause he's got three kids."

The image of the Dallas Cowboys is of this impersonal, cold machine. All business and no warmth. Nobody cares about anything except winning and losing. This image stems directly from Coach Landry's demeanor on the sidelines on Sunday. The TV cameras catch him prowling the sidelines with that blocked hat and chiseled profile right out of Dick Tracy. But let me tell you, it's a false image.

People see Landry on Sunday and whether the Cowboys are winning or losing, whether they just scored a big touchdown or turned the ball over inside their own 10-yard line, Landry's expression and manner never change.

Dan Reeves told me, "Since I've become a head coach, I respect Coach Landry more than ever. I always wondered why he was so emotionless. Why he didn't yell when we scored or scream when something went wrong. He looked at the play and went right back to what he was doing. I'm sitting on the sidelines and I'm calling the plays now here in Denver and at first I'd be hollering and screaming at people when they did something wrong. Then I'd look up and the thirty-second clock would be down to ten seconds and I hadn't called a play yet. It didn't take me long to realize you can't do that. You have to separate yourself from what's happening on the field. Once it's happened, that's it. Griping about it or cheering about it—that's for the fans."

A coach has to really discipline himself not to get caught up emotionally in the game. And that's hard to do because football is an exciting game. It gets you excited playing it or watching it. And coaches are human too. They'd love to scream for a big touchdown run.

It's not a personality flaw in Landry that he shows no emotion on the sidelines. He's not cold. He's under control. He'd love to go nuts but if he wants to do what's best for the team, if he wants to win, he can't.

They say football is a game of emotion but Landry didn't encourage you to be emotional on the field. But he didn't discourage it either. Landry wasn't big on pep talks. His approach was to do whatever he thought was necessary to get ready for the game and get the players ready. He would teach you everything there was to know about your opponent that week and give you a game plan that would beat that opponent. He figured if you did your job, you'd win. And your job was to play football. So if he had to give you a pep talk to get you to do your job, then you shouldn't be there.

Every once in a long while he'd chew us out a little at halftime if we had really played lousy. But most of the time if things weren't going right he'd come in at the half and try and fix it. If the offense was having trouble, he'd go in and meet with the offense. "They didn't do exactly what we thought, so let's do this." And he'd get out the chalkboard and draw up some plays.

Sometimes if we were really stinking up the field he might come in and say, "The game plan is good. You're just not executing." But he never yelled, "Kill! Win! Kill!"

Landry didn't like flash either. Just get the job done and let's go home. I led the team in receptions one year. We ran a lot of screens and flares and safety-valve kinds of stuff. And I loved to catch the ball. Maybe just a little too much.

One game I ran a little out pattern in the end zone. Morton threw the ball to me and I was wide open. Nobody within 10 yards of me. So I just reached up and snagged it one-handed. We used to catch one-handed all the time in practice and it was kind of a reflex. I just reached up and pulled it in, cool as can be.

So the next Monday when we were watching films, Landry runs that play by and stops the film. "That's a good catch, Walt," he says. Then he turns around and looks at me. "But don't ever drop one."

Believe me, that's the last hotdog catch this cowboy ever made.

Tom was also a stickler for punctuality. One day we were meeting at a hotel and the meeting started at eight o'clock. It was right off the Central Expressway, which used to be the main thoroughfare in Dallas. Well, this one particular day a grain truck overturned on the expressway about two miles north of the hotel and tied up traffic forever.

Four or five of the players got to the meeting about twenty minutes late. And so did Jim Myers, the assistant head coach. Well, Jim is real tight with a dollar and the fine was $150 and that included coaches. Jim was trying to explain the problem to Coach Landry.

"Hey, god dang, a grain truck overturned. You shouldn't fine these guys. Or me."

And Tom said, "You gotta plan for that."

Plan for flat tires. Plan for congestion. That was it. Period.

In the nine years I played, I never saw Landry late for a meeting or anything else. Never. Now you know over a nine-year period something had to have gone wrong. So that meant he even planned for *disasters*!

Actually, Tom Landry's got a great personality. He's not at all like his media image. But I've got sort of the same relationship with Tom that I've got with Staubach. I love the guy but I don't spend much time with him.

It goes back to interests. Tom's interests and mine aren't the same. We wouldn't pal around together even if we had the time. He don't like to go to the beer joint. He don't dance to country music. He don't ride a horse and he don't want to rope steers. I don't even know what all Tom does in his spare time. I know he plays golf and talks about football and, oh ya, he's definitely a churchgoing man.

Coach was big in the Fellowship of Christian Athletes. Landry had a devotional every Sunday before a game. But it wasn't one of those deals where you had to attend. If you wanted to go, you'd go. And plenty of people showed up. Hell, I believe in God. I was raised to go to church and it was kinda nice really. You'd go to the devotional, get a little peace of mind, eat a pregame meal and then try to cripple forty other human beings.

Some of the speakers Tom brought in were really good. Some were ex-football players who had gone into the ministry and, man, they could sell that Bible. I remember he had a guy come in once who was a gospel singer. The guy had been on dope and robbed banks and ended up doing a good stretch in prison. So he got up and talked to us about, "Once you're bad, you can go good." Something like that. I'm not exactly sure what it was. Nobody ever listened. But the guy was a hell of a good singer, I remember that.

Ya, Tom was a very religious man. Buddy Dial used to call him the Reverend T.L. But above all Tom was a practical man. He knew you could pray all you wanted but if you can't play football you're gonna get your ass beat on Sunday. Amen.

Landry enjoyed fun up to a point. As long as it didn't interfere with business. Because he was all business. Especially on Sunday. But Tom'd go along with a practical joke as long as it didn't interfere with practice.

I don't know what it was but I always seemed to be the guy who was pulling the practical jokes on Tom. When I look back on it, it doesn't seem like the smartest move I ever made considering the kind of talent I had.

Landry's birthday fell during the season and it was traditional that someone would go get a cake for Tom and have it sent over. We'd be in a meeting and they'd come in there with the cake. And everybody'd be making snide remarks under their breath. "Ah, who gives a shit." Stuff like that.

They'd cut the cake and hand it out. It was all business. Grim, serious stuff. They'd sing "Happy Birthday," then, "OK, get the cake outta here. Now where were we?"

Well, one year Lilly gets up and says, "Today is Coach Landry's birthday and we got a special guest to come in today to present the cake to Coach."

And Tom looks over and through the door walks this deformed VA hospital dischargee. Horribly disfigured with no hair and a swollen head. He was wearing a blue VA hospital robe with nothing on underneath, just those two hairy legs sticking out under his robe. Of course, it's me.

I had this mask that was so real, so lifelike it was frightening. It was the ugliest, most gruesome thing you ever saw. The eerie part was you could see the eyes move which made it positively grotesque.

When Landry saw this guy he nearly had a stroke. He hits the podium and knocks it down trying to get out of the way and staggers back to the wall.

Normally Tom would say, "Hi, how are you? Sorry about your face."

You know, polite small talk. Present the stiff upper lip. Do good for the community. But this mask was so hideous, so real-looking, Landry just staggered back with his mouth hanging open.

I stumbled up with the cake and started picking my nose and scratching my ass, sitting there staring at Landry with this cake in my hands. And Landry is up against the wall with this horrified look on his face.

Then everybody started laughing and Tom just blushed and broke out in a big sweat. It was the most flustered I'd ever seen Landry. It took fifteen, twenty minutes before he could get back to the X's and O's. Which was a record for sure. The Russians could drop the A-bomb on Dallas and Landry'd still be preparing for the Redskins.

Then there was the time I nearly blew Tom's brains out. I had a friend called Gene Goss who owned a used-car lot out on Ross Avenue. Goss was an institution in Dallas.

"Goss on Ross." "Gene Goss the tradin hoss."

Goss was a crazy sonuvabitch. He had a sign out front: "We guarantee our cars 30 days or 30 feet whichever comes first."

And next to that:

NEW CARS—$89.50 DOWN.
USED CARS—$79.50 DOWN.
GET TO WORK CARS—$69.50 DOWN.
GET TO WORK LATE CARS—$59.50 DOWN.
WORK CARS FOR TEMPORARY JOBS—$49.50 DOWN.

Goss had this old car with a pipe welded through the floorboard between the driver's seat and the passenger seat that led down to the ground. He had a cap on it and a little hole in it so you could light a cherry bomb and drop it down there and scare the shit out of anyone within a mile.

I drove it to practice one rainy day and pulled into Landry's parking place right next to the door. Tom comes into the training room where I'm getting taped and he's a little soggy because he had to park about twenty cars down and walk in the rain.

"Walt."

"Yes, sir."

"Is that your car out there in my place?"

"Ya, it is."

It was raining like hell so we weren't gonna practice for a while so I told him, "Come on out, Coach, and let me show you this baby."

We walked out there and I'm smoking a cigar and I jump in the car and fire the engine up.

"Boy, that's nice," Landry says and he's listening to the engine. And I drop that cherry bomb down there and *kaboom!* Landry jumps about nine miles. He couldn't hear a thing the rest of the day.

"Coach, what route you want me to run on this play?"

"Huh?"

Coach had a good sense of humor but some things would go right over his head. He just wouldn't get it. Especially anything that had to do with the team, he found very little humor in.

One time Tom got up and gave us this big talk about how he always coached better when he had oatmeal as his pregame meal. Now most of the Cowboys liked to eat a big breakfast on game day. Even Cliff Harris would eat a huge breakfast even though right afterward he'd throw it right back up again because he was so nervous.

We were in New York that week to play the Giants and one of the trainers starts the morning roll call. You've got to stand up and make your presence known and tell them what you want for breakfast.

"Adderley."

"Oatmeal!"

"Andrie."

"Oatmeal!"

"Bruenig."

"Oatmeal!"

"Cole."

"Oatmeal!"

Everybody ordered oatmeal. And Tom didn't even flinch. He never realized it was a joke. We all had to go up to the trainer afterward and tell him to cancel the forty orders of mush. Who the hell could face the New York Giants on a bowl of oatmeal?

Duane Thomas was nearly Tom Landry's downfall.

Landry was always distant with his players. Not by nature but by plan. He didn't want to get too close to a player because he knew someday he might have to trade him or cut him. And he didn't want his feelings to interfere with his judgment about what was best for the team.

That's not his personality though. Landry cared about his players. He cared about your problems on and off the field. If you had problems outside of football, he wanted to know about it. If he could help, he would. Every trade he made, every time he cut somebody, it bothered him. I think it was on his mind for a long, long time. But I think he tried to put his feelings aside and do what was best for the team every time.

Hell, now that I'm retired he'll come up and holler at me. He's friendly as hell. But back then he treated you strictly as an employee doing a job. If you did the job for him, you had a job. If you didn't do the job, somebody else would. He never played favorites. The word "favorite" was not in his vocabulary.

Until Duane Thomas came along.

Duane Thomas was pro football's Jekyll and Hyde. Duane played for Dallas for two years and in that time he established himself as the premier running back in football and also the premier pain in the ass.

Now Duane was an outstanding talent, that was for sure. He was a hell of a running back filled with natural ability. He could run with power and speed. He was smooth as silk when he ran and he had moves that had linebackers grabbing for air. He'd just lope along and suddenly he'd be through a hole and gone.

Plus, I believe Duane was a genuinely nice person. In his rookie year you couldn't have asked for a more cooperative, soft-spoken guy. He worked hard and he was nice as hell to everybody.

In his second year he wouldn't talk to anyone. He just stalked around brooding. Bob Hayes nicknamed him "Othello."

I honestly don't think anyone knows why he didn't talk. I don't think even Duane knew. He probably got some bad advice. But whatever it was, he just wouldn't talk to anybody. And I mean nobody! Not just the press or the fans. He wouldn't talk to anybody on the *team* either. Not the coaches, not the players, not the other running backs. Nobody.

When they took roll call at team meetings, he wouldn't answer when his name was called. When Tom asked him why, Duane said, "You can see me. I'm sitting right there."

Thomas hurt himself in a game once and Jethro Pugh came over and asked him, "How's the knee?" Duane said, "Why you wanna know? You a doctor?"

He was a horse's ass.

Thomas *must* have been talking to somebody—his mother or somebody. But I never saw it. Hell, he wouldn't even talk to the stewardesses on the team plane. And *everybody* tries to talk to the stewardesses.

People always asked me, "How did you and Duane get along?" Well, I liked Duane. I always liked him. I liked him when he was weird. I didn't give a damn if he ever talked because he played. That son of a bitch played. And I don't say that even about a lot of guys who did talk.

One time Duane scored a touchdown against San Francisco in a play-off game in Texas Stadium. They called an audible at the goal line and Duane went to the wrong side of the formation. I told him, "Duane, other side." He moved over. They pitched out to him and he scored a TD.

A writer asked me after the game, "Did you line up in the wrong spot?" And I said, "Yes."

They found out later that I lied to them and they came back. "Why didn't you tell us Thomas was lined up in the wrong spot?"

"Because y'all been on his ass all year."

Hey, I liked the guy.

Actually, Duane and I did talk. We played in the same backfield so we had to talk because backs got to talk. You can't play in the same backfield unless you do. You'd be running all over each other. So there's a lot of talk that goes on between backs when they break the huddle, set up and when they call audibles or when the defenses change alignments. If you don't talk, it don't work.

Of course I never talked to him before or after the game. But during the game we talked plenty.

I never had any real problem with Duane except in practice. He'd stand off by himself during practice. And sometimes he'd practice and sometimes he wouldn't. Oh, Duane would run with the first-team offense. But then when it came time for the defense to practice, he'd refuse to run. We'd all run on the dummy teams to simulate the opponent's offense. If you had three backs, you'd run every third play. But Duane wouldn't do it, which put an extra load on me and the other running backs. And that pissed us off.

I got my ass chewed out in practice one day because it was Duane's turn to run a dummy play and he was off dicking around as usual. "What the hell's wrong with Thomas?" I yelled.

Landry jumped all over me, then he said, "It's your turn to run. Get in there." Oh, that went over big with the rest of the veterans.

The worst part of it was that Landry let him get away with it. Anybody else would have gotten the boot. You don't want to practice? Goodbye. But not Duane Thomas. Landry left him alone. So while the rest of us kicked butt during practice, Duane stood over on the sidelines chewing gum. And Landry didn't say shit.

I'm not sure of Landry's motivation. He knew Duane had some kind of problem. He didn't know what it was but

Tom's the kind of guy who cares about people. There's no telling how many hours and days and weeks and months Tom spent on Duane trying to straighten him out. And I think Landry looked at Duane as his one big failure. He wanted to get Duane back on the right track. Tom wanted to save him, wanted to give him a chance to get back to being a human being again.

But it didn't work.

That's when Landry really lost the respect of the veteran players. Because all of a sudden we now had a double standard. Landry had never had one set of rules for one guy and another set for everybody else. You performed, you fit in, you went by the rules—or you were gone, baby. Guys like Bob Lilly and Lee Roy Jordan and Chuck Howley—every one of them had been All-Pro for years and Landry never so much as let them take an extra piss during practice.

Ironically, Landry's failure with Duane showed the strength of his character. It showed how much he really did care about his players. Most other coaches would have gotten rid of Thomas right away if he'd given them that kind of trouble. And, in fact, they did. After he left Dallas, Thomas was traded to team after team, even though everybody knew he was one of the best backs in football.

If Landry was truly like his image—cold, calculating, humorless and unemotional—he would have cut Thomas without a second thought.

Duane ran us right into the Super Bowl that year and it just about destroyed the team. A Super Bowl is supposed to bring everybody together and here we were holding up the Super Bowl trophy and everybody is pissed off.

In the end I thought the whole thing was sad. When I look back at football what I miss the most is the other players. The closeness that you develop with forty guys over a nine-year period of time. It's a team sport so you better like other people.

Duane Thomas was at odds with his teammates. And here was one of the greatest pure talents ever to come along and he had two good years, then bounced around from team to team for three, four years not doing much of anything.

Then he was gone.

CHAPTER FIVE

JOE DON

Any coach will tell you that to succeed any system has to have great personnel. But with a great system if you get those great players, you'll insure success.

That was Landry's idea from the beginning.

From 1966 to 1983 nobody had a better record than Dallas. Nobody went to five Super Bowls and nobody consistently dominated their conference like the Cowboys. They were the New York Yankees of football. They won week after week, year after year.

And to do that you gotta have players. Man, I was surrounded by some talent when I played for Dallas. Some of the best football players ever put on the same field at the same time. Guys like Bob Lilly, Don Meredith, Roger Staubach, Lee Roy Jordan, Chuck Howley, Ralph Neely and Bob Hayes were among the best ever to play their positions. Ever.

The first piece in Landry's championship puzzle was Don Meredith. Since Dallas was not organized in time to participate in the 1960 draft, Chicago Bears' owner George

Halas had agreed to select Meredith in the first round and then swap his rights to the Cowboys for their third-round draft choice in the next draft. This little maneuver wasn't a charity deal. It was done in order to keep Dandy Don out of the clutches of the rival AFL.

Landry now had the centerpiece, the guy he planned to build his offense around.

I believe Meredith was the greatest quarterback Dallas ever had, including Staubach. Roger got mad at me when he read in the paper that I'd said that. But I still believe it. Don Meredith was simply one of the greatest natural-born leaders ever to play football. As far as knowing the game and knowing how to lead men, nobody could touch Meredith.

Also, Don was a great athlete. He was a high school All-American in basketball and football. When he retired he took up golf and now he's about a 4-handicap golfer. Whatever he tried, he was good at.

Meredith had a great arm yet he could scramble too. He had the ability to throw the ball on the run and hit his man. Before he was through, Don passed for over 17,000 yards and hit over 50 percent of his passes. His greatest asset though was his charisma. He'd step into a huddle and you just had the feeling the guy was gonna get the job done.

He'd call a play you'd bet your mother wouldn't work but when Don Meredith called it, it sounded like the greatest play ever drawn up.

But for most of his career at Dallas he didn't have anybody to help him. When he joined the Cowboys, Dallas was an expansion team in its first year. Don backed up little Eddie LaBaron for a while that year. Then they threw him to the dogs. And Don got chewed up for five years until Landry was able to build a team around Meredith. Then there was no stopping Dallas. But until then it was definitely the dog days for Don and the Cowboys.

Meredith was like nobody else they ever had at Dallas. Or probably ever will. In a word, Joe Don was cool. When I was a rookie in 1966, we took a plane ride out of New York after our first play-off game ever. After you're a veteran, you get to sit at the back of the plane. All the steak eaters sit in the front. If you're big-time press you sit in first class with all the coaches and the front-office guys—Tex Schramm and Gil Brandt and Clint Murchison. The lesser crowd sits in the first two or three rows of coach. Then the rookies take up the next few rows sitting three to a row. The back third of the plane is where the veterans sit and they sit *two* to a row. The back is the preferred seating because the players want to sit as far away from the coaches and the press as possible.

Well, we're at the back of the plane. I'm on the aisle and Meredith and Gent are sitting in the last row of the plane where they always sit. Joe Don is sittin there drinkin him a beer, smokin a cigarette.

It was snowing like shit and this sonuvabitch takes off and the whole plane shudders. It sounded like a bomb went off. BOOM! They tried climbing again and BOOM!

We'd been sitting on the ground for about two hours while they deiced the plane three or four times and, in the meantime, Lilly musta drank a case of beer. So Lilly was ripped. Lilly stands up in the aisle and says, "We've all had it, baby. It's allllll over." And he's still chugging his beer.

The plane is flying at about a 45-degree angle because they can't get its ass in the air and all Lilly's beer cans start rolling down the aisle. One of the stewardesses comes skidding down the aisle on her hands and knees. The beer cans are flying by her and she's screaming, "We're in trouble! We're in trouble!"

"Oh, no!"

Everybody is scared to piss. Pete Gent yells, "Joe Don, Joe Don! We're gonna crash!"

But Meredith is just sitting there and, finally, he takes a long drag off his cigarette and a big swig of beer and he says, "Well, it's been a good un, ain't it."

Now that's cool.

I'm thinking, "It's been a good one? What the hell are you talking about? We're gonna die!"

But Meredith never even blinked. He just kept sipping his beer. He could have cared less if that plane went down. I tell you, if I'd known we weren't gonna die, I'd have said something cool too. But I didn't think we were gonna make it. Nobody did. They were so scared they didn't even try to pretend they weren't scared. Afterward everybody said, "I was scared shitless."

Except Meredith. He actually didn't care. And everybody knew he wasn't bullshittin either.

I was always scared to death of flying anyway. In my rookie year we had a flight and I'm up front next to the wing, staring out at the engine. I'm kinda mesmerized, just listening to the hum of the engine. And Meredith comes up to me and says, "Hey, Walt."

"Ya, Joe Don."

"You been sittin there for about an hour and a half. Don't you need to go to the bathroom?"

"Oh, yes, sir, I do."

"Well," he said, "get up and go. I'll watch the engine for you."

Don had such a carefree attitude about life, you just had to love the guy. One night me and Meredith went out drinking. He started the night with four one-hundred-dollar bills in his wallet. As the night progressed he bought about everybody he saw a beer and he went through the whole wad. All $400—which was a hell of a lot of money back then. Especially to a boy from Lewisville.

"God darn, Meredith," I said, "how can you afford to blow all that dough?"

"Whadda ya mean," he said, "I just made four hundred dollars."

"How do you figure that?"

"Hell, I had eight-hundred-dollars worth of fun."

More than anything, Meredith was just a simple country boy who loved to have a laugh. I teamed up with a guy named David Dickerson. Brainy Dave they called him. We were an act. I'd walk into a bar with a mouth full of lighter fluid and strike a match and *woooooooooooo-roooooooaarrrr!* Looked like a goddamn dragon, flames'd shoot out about six feet. Then Dave would take two beer bottles and crack! crack! he'd break them across his head. They used to call Brainy Dave and me to do parties and stuff.

Well, Meredith just loved this act. He used to wake me up, "Come on, come on, come on, wake up, get up, get up!" And he'd drag me upstairs at the dorm where the rookies were sleeping. There would be three of those poor rooks sound asleep in a room after a grueling day of practice and dodging the Turk.

"OK, do it, do it!" Don'd whisper. He'd crack the door and I'd load up and *woooooooooooooo-roooooooooaaaarrr!* This big ball of fire would shoot across the room right above their beds as they were sleeping. And all you'd see is these eyes wide open, scared shitless. *"Ahhhhhhhhhhhhhhhhhhhhhhhhhhhh-hhh!"*

"That's good, Walt," Meredith would say. "Next room."

Got to be a ritual. The rookie roast.

Ya, Don was cool. And that's part of what made him a great quarterback. He'd come strolling into the huddle humming a country tune, "I Didn't Know God Made Honky Tonk Angels."

Meredith never let his teammates get tight. Especially before a big game. The night before the NFL championship game against Green Bay in 1966, word got around that Meredith was hurt. The game the next day was not only for the title but for the right to go to Super Bowl I.

We always had a team meeting the night before a game at the hotel where we were staying. And when I got to the meeting that night everything's very quiet. It's like a morgue. I sat down and somebody whispered to me, "You see what happened to Meredith?"

"No."

"He went through a plate-glass window when he was out shopping today."

"What!"

"Ya. He cut himself up real bad and he's not gonna be able to play tomorrow."

Meredith comes in about that time and sits down. You could see he was completely dejected. His head's hung down real low. And there was this big bloody scar across his face. It was gruesome. My heart just stopped when I saw him because our chances of winning suddenly weren't very good anymore.

Coach Landry got up and made his talk, told us what we had to do to win the ball game. When he got through, Meredith got up and we all figured he was gonna give us a little talk about how we could win the game without him or some other bullshit we wouldn't believe.

And, yank! He just peeled this ugly bloody scar off his face. He'd had some Hollywood makeup guy he knew come in and put this damn thing on him. It looked so real you wanted to throw up when you looked at it.

The whole place just exploded with laughter. Sigmund Freud couldn't have done a better job of relaxing us. Here we were a young expansion team, first time in the playoffs and we were going to face Lombardi's Packers. And Meredith just turned it all into a big joke. And the next day we went out and played a hell of a ball game.

. . .

It never surprised me that Don made it big on *Monday Night Football* and later as an actor on TV and in movies. He was a natural-born celebrity. Whether he walked into a beer joint or a black-tie affair, Joe Don was the center of attention. And if he wasn't when he got there, he would be within a couple minutes. That's just the way it was. Don didn't plan it that way. That was his style. He was a quarterback on and off the field. He ran the show and everybody followed. And if there wasn't any show going, he'd make one. Whatever it took. He'd get up and sing, tell old stories, dance. He's exactly the same way today.

Meredith was a true celebrity and there weren't many real celebrities in football—a guy who could hold the spotlight even when he wasn't on the field. Now Joe Namath was a celebrity. Broadway Joe. He was single and good-looking so all the unmarried women and most of the married ones loved him. He owned a bar and he was a great football player. He told everybody he was going to beat the world champion Colts in Super Bowl III and he went out and did it. That's the kind of stuff charisma is made of.

Roger Staubach was a celebrity too, but for exactly the opposite reasons as Namath. He wasn't flashy. He was cut from the military cloth. "Yes, sir." "No, sir." He was the family, go-to-church type which a lot of people relate to. And he was exciting as hell to watch.

As a football player I never looked at myself as a celebrity because I knew a lot of real football celebrities and I saw what their life was like. A guy like Namath couldn't go anywhere or he'd get mobbed. See, I could go anywhere I wanted. People would recognize me but they didn't care. "Oh, ya, there's Walt. Hope he don't want to come over and talk to us because we seen him play. And he sure as hell don't know nothin bout football."

My only real shot at fame was my guest spot on *The David Letterman Show*. I was gonna get up there and tell a few Wild West stories and a couple lies about my football prowess and then I was gonna rope a mechanical steer they had rigged up.

But even that one fleeting moment of fame never came off.

David and I were talking before the show and he said he was gonna save me for last. Problem was he had some has-been starlet on before me. You could tell she'd been on lots of talk shows before because he couldn't shut her up. Everything he said she jumped right in and did five minutes on it.

Finally, late in the show Letterman comes backstage and says, "Walt, I'm sorry. I got two minutes left and I don't want to put you on for two minutes. Please come back and I'll get you on first next time."

"You got it," I said.

So I take the limo back to the suite they got me at the Essex House on Central Park. When I walk into my room there's a half gallon of Scotch which is older than my daddy and a note from Letterman: "Sorry you didn't get on. She's still talking. David."

I drank most of that half gallon that night and after that I was always a big fan of Letterman's.

Now some people can handle their celebrity. I thought I handled it pretty good at the time—the little bit I had. But looking back on it, I don't think I did.

I never thought I was trying to be somebody special. I didn't think I had a big head. But I came to expect things. You expect the best table in a restaurant. You expect to be welcomed anywhere. Just because of who you are. That ain't the way it's supposed to be. But movie stars and professional athletes come to expect special treatment after a while. Because that's the way they get treated.

When you travel in the off-season, you find yourself making sure you got a Dallas Cowboys' sticker on your bags. Or you go into a bar and you've got your Super Bowl ring on and nobody's made a big deal out of you (and they've had plenty of chances). Finally you say something like, "Damn, it's hot in here. I think I'll take my ring off."

Now I don't often agree with Barry Switzer, the Oklahoma University football coach, but he once said something I thought was brilliant. "Some people are born on third base and go through life thinking they hit a triple." And that's the way some celebrities act. Life treated them good and they think it's their own fault.

I try to be nice to everyone but I tell you it's tough sometimes. Not too long ago a guy walked up to me. I don't know him from Adam and he says, "Hey, Walt, what're you growing that ugly-ass beard for?"

"Same reason you're growing that ugly-ass moustache, I guess."

And the guy was offended.

A lot of other times a guy has walked up to me and said, "Are you Walt Garrison?"

"Ya, that's me."

"Nooooooo, you're not. You're too little to be Walt Garrison. He was six foot two and two hundred and twenty something."

"No, I'm Walt Garrison."

"No, you're not."

"OK, I'm not."

And then he'll turn around to his friends and say, "See, I told you he wasn't Walt Garrison."

Happens all the time.

. . .

Now, Meredith was a guy who really knew how to handle celebrity. He was comfortable with it and he really enjoyed it. When Don was still a big star on *Monday Night Football,* he and I went to a bar and people began to gather looking for autographs.

"I'm with my friend Walt here," Meredith said politely. "We ain't seen each other in a long time. We just want to spend the evening together. But I'll be here tomorrow morning at nine o'clock and I'll sign all the autographs you want."

So they cleared away and we had a peaceful dinner together. Then Don went down there the next morning and there musta been a couple hundred people lined up and he signed autographs and entertained them all for about two hours.

Simple as that. No muss, no fuss. And Don enjoyed the whole thing.

Meredith was just himself. That was his secret. My daddy always said, "Don't try to be something you ain't. Figure out what you are and try to be the best you can be at that."

Meredith didn't try to act country. He was country. He was from little bitty Mt. Vernon, Texas. With Meredith you got what you saw.

That's what I could never figure about Namath. Lee Roy Jordan and Joe were friends because they were teammates at Alabama for a couple years. We were down in Miami one year, so me and Lee Roy stopped by Joe's bar in Fort Lauderdale, The Bachelor's III.

Namath turned out to be the nicest guy you ever want to meet. Real country. He was from Pennsylvania but you'd never knew he grew up a Yankee. He talked country, dipped snuff and he played for Alabama. But when Namath was doing *Monday Night Football* they had him taking all these voice lessons. He sounded like a guy trying to learn a different language. He quit being a country boy and tried to be something else. And that never works.

Just what people saw and heard on *Monday Night Football* was the way Meredith really was. None of that was phony. That was the way the real Joe Don Meredith acted every day. The accent, the way he talked, the things he said, the singing, that was just him.

Howard Cosell said, "There was another more complicated Meredith." Meredith was a put on, he said. If anybody was a put on, it was Cosell. If a guy sitting on a crashing plane can say, "It's been a good un," it ain't no put on. You can't fake that.

Cosell didn't know what he was talking about. He wrote a book, *I Never Played The Game.* He didn't have to tell me. It was obvious. I always said Cosell had the greatest recollection of unimportant facts of anybody alive. Who gives a crap who the 1938 Yankee first, second and third basemen were when you're watching the second half of a football game?

I never said Cosell wasn't smart though. In fact, I only met him once at a restaurant in Buffalo, New York, and we visited for a while and I thought the guy was brilliant. And he's the one who really saved *Monday Night Football.*

A lot of people turned on *Monday Night Football* just to cuss Cosell. Bars had "I hate Cosell" contests. Whoever won got to throw a brick through the TV set at him. So a lot of people turned it on just to hear Meredith put Cosell down—the country boy putting down the city slicker.

Anyway, Meredith was going to quit the show the first year it was on because he didn't think he was any good. But Cosell told him, "Don't quit. You're exactly what we need. You be the good guy and I'll be the bad guy and we'll both end up millionaires."

And he didn't and they did.

.   .   .

Another thing. When Meredith was with the Cowboys the locker-room atmosphere was always great. The team spirit, the camaraderie between the players, black and white, was the best.

Most of that was due to Joe Don. He was the undisputed team leader. And just because of the way he was—friendly, up-front, easygoing and fun—we were always a happy team. After practice we'd go down to the beer joint and work out any problems we had. Meredith set that up. Thursday afternoon was official "beer joint day" because that was the last day of hard practice for the week. And everybody'd go down to the VIP Lounge, a bar off the Central Expressway. Meredith would get up and sing and drink and talk and drink and just generally hold court. "OK, what's wrong? Who's got a bitch?"

Everything would come out. I mean everything. Personal problems, team problems, problems with the coaches, other players, even their goddamn wives. Hell, we all knew before the wives did who was leaving whom. We'd talk and bitch and yell and drink some beer and it'd all come spilling out. And by the time it was all over, we'd all be laughing.

At six o'clock we'd just head over to the beer joint. Hell, I was afraid not to go. Everybody was there except Chuck Howley. But Howley never went beer drinking anytime. Never. He'd go on home to his family. Howley loved his family. And that was OK with everybody. He was an All-Pro linebacker who went to the Pro Bowl every year. If you're as good as Howley was, nobody cares what you do as long as you put on your uniform every Sunday. Nobody gave "Hogmeat" any shit.

Another thing we used to do that they cut out was the Sunday night party. Whether we played at home or away, as soon as the game was over, we'd head for the Falstaff Brewery. They had a Hospitality Room there and Zider Zee, a fish restaurant, would bring in fish, oysters, clams, shrimp—just all kinds of good stuff. And there'd be plenty of beer. And they had a little band and the team would party. It kept everyone close—win or lose.

Also, Monday was our day off and quite a few of us used to go hunting at Punk Helm's ranch out in Sulphur Springs. And once a year they'd have a big dove hunt and steak fry and they'd invite the Cowboys.

All that stuff kept us close as a team.

Nowadays, it's strictly a business. Immediately after practice the players take off because they've got all these outside business interests to take care of. Of course, when you're making half a million a year, you tend to have more outside interests than a guy making thirty or forty thousand.

Anyway, at these team meetings, Meredith used to love to get up and sing. Matter of fact, he actually cut a record one time. He sold four or five copies. I bought two of them and Meredith bought the other three. The A side was "Travelin' Man" and the flip side was "Them That Ain't Got It Can't Lose." A couple of classics.

If you drank a lot of beer Meredith started to sound pretty good. But it had to be a *lot* of beer because he was awful. When Meredith sang "Turn Out the Lights" on *Monday Night* that was his best. That was Joe Don at full throttle.

Buddy Dial was Meredith's roommate and he liked to sing a little too. Dial had come over from Pittsburgh a couple years before I got there. With the Steelers, Buddy teamed up with the great Bobby Layne and he turned out to be All-Pro four times and set several records that are still standing. On and off the field.

Dial was a funny guy. He was high all the time. It was like he was on dope or something but he never touched the stuff. Six o'clock in the morning, he'd get up and he was feeling great! When he went to bed, he was feeling great! The food was great! The beer was great! Life was great! Dial made Norman Vincent Peale look like a guy who just got a busy signal calling the suicide-prevention hotline.

Anyway, Buddy recorded a couple albums himself. He also had a song that got to be number one in the nation. It was called "Hey, Baby!" And that was nearly the entire extent of the lyrics. "Hey, baby. I wanna be your baby. Hey, baby, hey, baby, hey, baby."

That was it. The sucker was number one!

When the veterans arrived at training camp the first night, they would get the rookies up to sing. Usually the top draft choices. You sang your school song usually. A lot of the rookies would rehearse. They'd call on one guy and a bunch of them would get up there and they'd do routines like the Platters.

Along about the second night of my rookie year at camp it was my turn to sing. Meredith and Buddy Dial were Country and Western fans so they had me sing, "All Around the Water Tank." I knew a bunch of those old C&W songs. So Meredith would yell out, "Do you know such and such." And stupid me, I kept saying, "Oh, ya man, I know that song."

Now, most times a rookie would sing once or twice, maybe even three times if he was either real good or real bad. Never more than that. I sang every night for a week and a half. And it wasn't just one song. I'd sing for an hour. I had a regular gig going.

But the great thing about Meredith and Dial, after I'd get about halfway through the song, they'd get up there and sing it with me. They just loved country music.

I got tired of singing every night though and finally I found a way out. Don had been married and divorced. But he started dating his wife again and he ended up marrying her all over. But that didn't last too long either, so they ended up getting divorced again. They had a little daughter and Don was real sentimental about her.

Well, one night he picked up his daughter and they went out and when he came back he was feeling misty. Don had had a few drinks and so he tells me, "Come on, rookie, you gotta sing."

I told Reeves, "I'm gonna fix him now."

So I sang this song about a man who was divorced and took his daughter window shopping for Christmas. The whole bit. It was sad as hell and I had Meredith bawling his eyes out.

He never asked me to sing again.

A lot of the Cowboys were C&W fans and we got to collecting funny lines or titles from country songs. Stuff like, "If fingerprints showed up on skin, wonder whose I'd find on you?" Or, "I've got the hungries for your love, and I'm waiting in your welfare line."

We started to put them down on paper and the first year there were two or three pages of these little nuggets. It got longer and longer and Doug Todd, the PR guy for the team, finally made the damn thing into a book. Here's some of my favorites from the original "list."

"I bought the shoes that just walked out on me."

"If you want to keep the beer real cold, put it next to my ex-wife's heart."

"How come my dog don't bark when he comes a-round?"

"I gave her a ring and she gave me the finger."

"Thank God and Greyhound you're gone."

"Don't cry down my back, baby, you might rust my spurs."

"Don't tell me you're sorry. I know how sorry you are."

"It took a hell of a man to take my Ann but it sure didn't take him long."

"I wouldn't take you to a dogfight, baby, even if I thought you could win."

"How many women have become a sinner thinking they were gonna get a roast beef dinner?"

"Did I fall out of her favor because the only ring I ever gave her was the one she scrubbed out of the tub?"

"When I'm alone I'm in bad company."

"I don't know whether to kill myself or go bowling."

"My wife ran off with my best friend and I miss him."

"Drop-kick me, Jesus, through the goalposts of life."

CHAPTER SIX

DOOMSDAY

When you think of the Dallas Cowboys of the sixties and seventies, most people think of the great offenses that we had. Those exciting, point-a-minute teams. "Speed Inc." they called us, with Meredith throwing those long bombs to Bob Hayes and Lance Rentzel. And Don Perkins and Calvin Hill and Duane Thomas chewing up yards out of the backfield.

But the defense at Dallas was even better than the offense. The Cowboys could always score big with Landry drawing up those plays for Meredith and Staubach. But until Tom put together that great defense we didn't win any championships.

"The Doomsday Defense" they called it. Chuck Howley, Lee Roy Jordan, Cornell Green, Mel Renfro, Charlie Waters, Cliff Harris, Jethro Pugh and the big boy in the middle—Bob Lilly.

Of any single player, Bob Lilly had the most to do with the success of the Cowboys. Lilly was the key to the success of the Flex Defense because the Flex counts on the play of one dominant tackle on the line to make it work. His job is to try to use his speed and quickness to beat the "choke" block—when the offensive guard pulls and the center tries to block back for the guard, tries to "choke" the hole.

Lilly could beat that block with ease. He was simply the quickest defensive lineman ever to play the game. Before the center could take one step, Lilly was by him. His ability to get off the line of scrimmage at the snap of the ball was awesome. The center would snap the ball and try to block Lilly and he couldn't touch him. Bob'd be past him standing in the other team's backfield. A lot of times Lilly would get to the quarterback before he had time to hand off to the running back.

So they couldn't pull the guard on Lilly because it was like an invitation for Bob to cremate the quarterback. That eliminates about 40 percent of a team's offense right there.

Lilly made the Flex possible. Most 4–3 linemen sit back and try to read the offense. But in the Flex, Lilly's job was to create havoc. He had to control his gap but as soon as something happened, he could take off. And Lilly was awesome at screwing up an offense before it could get out of its tracks.

The only reason Lilly could do what he did was because he was the most physically talented defensive lineman ever to play football. He was the best. Take Randy White, the Cowboys' perennial All-Pro defensive tackle. He's a slam-dunk lock to make the Hall of Fame. He's quick as hell and his strength is legendary. Ask anybody who knows anything about football and they'll tell you White is the best defensive lineman in football. But he doesn't have the size or the strength that Lilly had. Lilly was 6'5" and 280 pounds and he could run down just about any running back from behind.

I've seen three guys try to block him on pass protection and Lilly'd just go by all three of them. He used to just amaze us. We'd be watching films the following week and Lilly'd go right through two, three huge linemen like they were mannequins and we'd all shake our heads in amazement.

The incredible part about Lilly is it was all natural with him. He never lifted weights. He never worked out or ate a special diet or anything. Bob Lilly was born to play football. He'd walk out on the field and say, "OK, let's play some ball."

He was like some damn animal, like a wild lion out on the savannah in Africa. Just born that way. They put him on the football field and he'd just eat people alive.

Before Lilly was through he was All-Pro seven times, played in the Pro Bowl every year he was in the league, made the Hall of Fame in a walk and was Dallas's first inductee into its Ring of Honor.

Bob Lilly could do just about whatever he wanted—on and off the field.

Lilly was the only guy I knew who hurt his back every year in the first two or three days of training camp. An injury that you couldn't find. But he'd report to the trainer and they'd send him to the team doctor. Lilly'd say he hurt his back and he'd walk around in his sweats until two-a-day workouts were over. The first week he wouldn't hardly come to practice at all. He'd stand around in his sweats and maybe walk a little. Three or four days later he'd start jogging. Then he'd run a little bit—if the spirit moved him. Just about the time the first preseason game'd roll around, he'd be in his pads ready to go.

That first game he'd play about a quarter. Next game he'd play a quarter and a half. The game after that he'd play a half. Until, finally, when the regular season started he was ready to go. That's the way Lilly did it. He just played himself into shape. And he was so good nobody gave a damn because they knew when they snapped the first ball Lilly'd be ready. What were they gonna do? Cut Bob Lilly? He's been All-Pro ten years in a row! "Well, we're sorry. Bob wasn't at practice, so we had to cut him."

Ya, Mr. Lilly had a free rein.

Bob was always getting pissed off at the coaches and they never said diddly to him.

"You're looking at the new Bob Lilly." That was his favorite expression. There were a hundred reincarnations of the "New Bob Lilly." When Bob would start up, we'd be whispering under our breath, "You mean the new *old* Bob Lilly."

Anyway, Lilly would go stomping through the plane on the way home. "You're looking at the new Bob Lilly. I ain't takin any more of their crap. They can kiss my ass. I'm mad now. I don't like the way they're doing things around here. Screw those goddamn coaches!"

"Jesus, Bob, they're right up there in first class." The rest of us weren't All-Pro every year and we were just a little bit afraid.

"I don't give a good goddamn. Those sons of bitches don't know shit."

Lilly was an eccentric and he had cranky opinions and ideas. He always had a "theory" about everything. And he wasn't shy about letting anybody and everybody know about it. And when Bob Lilly spoke, people pretended to listen.

Lilly used to punt every day before practice. He said, "I got it figured. It depends on how hard you throw the football down at your foot. It's like a baseball pitcher and a batter. If that sonuvabitch throws that thing at ninety mph, you don't have to swing that hard for it to go a mile. To hell with dropping the football down at your foot. You gotta *slam* that baby down."

Lilly was crazy. He'd punt every goddamn day. Boom! Boom! Boom!

"You gotta have stronger arm strength to kick those long balls," he'd rave. And he'd kick and kick and kick and kick and the goddamn ball wouldn't go 20 yards. That didn't bother Lilly. He had a theory and he *knew* it would revolutionize kicking. And he was gonna perfect it. Boom! Boom! Boom!

"You gotta get your arm strength up." Boom! Boom! Boom! And he'd throw it harder.

Never worked, of course.

Lilly's constant companion was George Andrie. Andrie was a 6'7", 255-pound giant who played the end next to Lilly in the Doomsday Defense. An unknown out of Marquette, Andrie played twelve years for the Cowboys and eventually became a damn good defensive end.

George was very intense on the field but he was a pussycat off it. He was the perfect running mate for Lilly. Bob needed someone who would listen to his dumb-ass theories. When Bob started spouting off, George would nod his head.

"George, you know what I think?"

"I don't know, Bob. Whadda you think?" That was Andrie. He was always asking Lilly what he thought. And Bob would roll on about some bitch he had or some new way to fix up the world.

Back when Bob was still drinking, he and George got drunk in Miami the night before a game. They were three stories up at this hotel and the swimming pool was right below their room.

Lilly said, "George, you think you can jump in that swimming pool?"

"I don't know, Bob, I don't know. Whadda you think, Bob?"

"Well, I think you can make it, George."

"Ya, Bob. Ya, I think I probably can."

"Then why don't you try it?"

"Ya, OK, Bob."

So George jumps off the balcony but he didn't come even close to hitting the pool. He fell through an awning next to the pool. That's the only thing that saved his life. Went right through the awning and landed on a patio table and hurt his back a little. Played the next day like nothing had happened.

"Ya, Bob, I think I can play. Whadda you think, Bob?"

Actually, despite all his idiosyncrasies, Lilly was a very sensitive person. An artist type, really. He was a shy person who had a real awareness of other people's feelings and a keen eye for beauty. Lilly's living in Las Cruces, New Mexico, now and he owns a photography studio. That's what he always wanted to be—a photographer. Not the kind who takes family portraits or anything like that. Lilly used to go out and shoot landscapes or buzzards eating coyotes. Arty shit.

We'd go to the games and Lilly'd have nine cameras hanging around his neck. He looked like a Japanese tourist. Lilly took hundreds of pictures wherever he went and he saved them over the years. He had big boxes of them, all catalogued. A couple of years ago he put together a book of his photos that he took when he was with Dallas. It was called *Reflections*. He had pictures of Lee Roy Jordan taking a leak and Landry with his finger up his nose. Plus a lot of beautiful and poignant stuff.

Lilly was a piece of art all by himself.

Backing up Lilly was the greatest corps of linebackers ever to play the game—Lee Roy Jordan, Chuck Howley and Dave Edwards. Now there may have been greater individual backers like Green Bay's Ray Nitschke or New York's Sam Huff or Chicago's Dick Butkus. But I'm not even sure that's true. Jordan and Howley certainly could compare with any of those guys. One thing is for sure—no one ever put three better linebackers on the field at one time.

Lee Roy was the team captain. He was middle linebacker and they're usually the leaders of the defense. Sam Huff, Dick Butkus, Jack Lambert. The tough guy is in the middle, the guy that can make the big tackle when it's got to be made.

The Flex was designed to funnel the running back into the middle linebacker. The defensive linemen would fill the gaps and the only daylight that was left was filled by Lee Roy Jordan.

Lee Roy was a good athlete—strong and wiry but he wasn't too big. He usually played at 210 or 215 which is small for a middle linebacker. But he was very smart and he could really hit. Jordan was ferocious. Bear Bryant said, "If the ball carrier stayed in the stadium, Lee Roy Jordan would hit him."

Lee Roy was the most tenacious player I've ever been around. We'd play intrasquad games and the running backs would fasten their chin straps tight because Lee Roy tried to kill everybody. When he'd hit you your mouthpiece would fly outta your mouth. It didn't matter if it was his own teammates. He'd hit his grandmother if she had a helmet on. That's why we called him "Killer." Lee Roy just loved to kill you. Six days of the week I hated Lee Roy, but on Sunday, when he was on my side, I loved him like a brother.

Lee Roy was just a tough son of a bitch. The only guy I ran up against who was as tough as Lee Roy was Dick Butkus, the Bear Hall of Famer. Butkus always had an intimidating style. One time I busted through the line into Butkus's territory for a pretty good gain and he took me down after 6 or 7 yards. He got up mad and told me, "If you ever come this way again, I'm gonna bite your head off."

And I looked at him and said, "Well, if you do, it'll be the first damn time you ever had any brains in your head."

Butkus just stared at me real mean for a couple seconds, then he cracked up. Even then Dick had that crazy sense of humor that comes out in his TV commercials. Of course, just because he thought I was funny that didn't stop him from trying to bite my head off next time we ran at him.

The outside linebacker next to Lee Roy was Chuck Howley. Howley was a number-one draft choice of the Bears in 1957. But after a knee injury in 1959, Chuck sat out the 1960 season. The Bears wanted to trade Howley but nobody knew if he could come back and be as good as he was. So there weren't many takers. The Cowboys, however, could afford to take a chance back then because they sure couldn't get any worse. So they grabbed Chuck. And, bingo, Howley turned out to be All-Pro just about every year and ended up in the Ring of Honor with Lilly and the rest of the Dallas legends.

Howley was simply a great athlete. He was 6'4" and 235 pounds and lettered in *five* sports at West Virginia—football, track, platform diving, wrestling and gymnastics! He could literally do anything he wanted. He's the only guy I ever saw on the football field who could change directions in midair. He just reminded you of a big ol cat.

It's a good thing he was such a great athlete because he didn't know a thing about the Dallas defense. Howley had more common sense when it came to football than anybody I ever saw. But as far as knowing exactly where he was supposed to be and what he was supposed to do in Landry's defense, he didn't have a clue. Instead of Tom, he could have been playing for William and Mary. Didn't make no never mind to Howley. Wherever the ball went that's where you'd find Hogmeat.

But Howley made more big plays, more interceptions, more big tackles for losses and recovered more fumbles than anybody I ever saw. But he was never where he was supposed to be. He just chased the ball. And he was such a phenomenal athlete, he could outrun, outmuscle and outjump everybody in his way.

Since Howley didn't play his position, someone had to cover for his ass. Jordan used to laugh, "Hell, I was the one always covering Howley's man and they put Hogmeat in the Ring of Honor."

Lee Roy would call a defensive signal and, on the way out of the huddle, Lee Roy'd have to tell Chuck four times what the play was. And it still didn't matter. Whatever he saw, that's what Howley did.

Pat Toomay was a rookie and D. D. Lewis, who was playing middle linebacker at the time, called a "Jet" defense and Pat wasn't sure what to do. So as they were lining up he whispered to Howley, "Hogmeat, what'll I do?"

And Chuck says, "I don't give a shit what you do. Just stay outta my way."

The truth was Howley didn't know and he didn't care. He was like a rabid dog. As soon as they snapped the ball he was looking for someone to bite.

Me and Lee Roy roomed together and we were a lot alike. When we went to bed we went to bed to sleep. Not Hogmeat. He was the only human being I ever knew who never slept. Never. I had the misfortune of rooming with Howley for two or three games. He was like a hot electrical wire dancing around.

He'd snap on the TV as soon as we got in the room and he'd watch four channels at once. He'd speed switch the channels going through them like a machine gun *pfffft-pfffft-pfffft*. It was like no one else was around. Twenty-two seconds on this channel, then back over here and back over there. And it usually wasn't on a program. He'd be watching the commercials! Guy drove me nuts. I'd go to bed dizzy.

And Howley'd sit right on the edge of the bed like he was mesmerized and *pfffft-pfffft-pfffft.*

"Hey, Chuck, just put it on one station and let's go to bed."

"Oh, ya, ya, Walt." And *pfffft-pfffft-pfffft-pfffft.* All night long.

The strong-side linebacker was Dave Edwards. He was probably one of the greatest strong-side linebackers ever to play the game. Except nobody knew it. He had the bad luck of playing next to Lee Roy and Chuck his whole career. And nobody could keep Hogmeat and Killer off the All-Pro teams. They made it year after year after year. Since you couldn't have all three Dallas linebackers as All-Pro, Edwards was odd man out.

In the Flex the strong-side linebacker's main job is to control the line of scrimmage, especially against the sweep. They'd send the tight end and the pulling guards and everybody else at Dave and he'd just push them all inside where Lilly and Jordan and Howley were waiting to gobble em up. They couldn't get around Dave because he had the strongest pair of hands in football. Once he clamped those paws on someone, they was clamped.

Dave made Cornell Green an All-Pro when he was playing strong safety for us. See, it was Green's responsibility to cover the tight end. But there was never any tight end to cover because Edwards would never let the son of a bitch off the line. Dave'd get a hold of him and that was it. The guy couldn't go anywhere.

But Edwards never got any recognition. Everybody he played with and against knew he was great but he never got the ink. No ink. No All-Pro. No Hall of Fame. No Ring of Honor.

Another thing—Edwards was funny! After we won the Super Bowl, we played the College All-Stars the first exhibition game the following year. To prepare for the game we looked at game films of Nebraska because Bob Devaney, the Nebraska coach, was coaching the All-Stars.

Coach Landry was up at the chalkboard diagramming plays and he said, "Now when Nebraska's got the ball . . ."

And Edwards interrupts, "Wait a minute, Coach. Nebraska?"

"Oh, no," Landry says, "I meant the All-Stars."

"Thank God," Edwards says. "Ain't no way we can beat Nebraska."

Playing behind Edwards, Jordan and Howley were three All-Pro defensive backs—Mel Renfro, Herb Adderley and Cornell Green. Green was the anchor in the defensive secondary. Corny was a basketball star from Utah State who developed into one of the greatest defensive backs that Dallas ever had. He was so tall you couldn't throw over him. Hell, you had a power forward out there playing cornerback who could run and jump like Michael Jordan. He was awesome.

The amazing thing about Green is he played no college football at all and only one year of high school ball and that was on offense. The first game he played at Dallas was against the Green Bay Packers and when he went out there on the field to face Paul Hornung and Jim Taylor and Bart Starr he had never tackled anyone in a game.

"The whole game was like I was on a psychedelic trip," Corny said.

But Corny survived his hallucinations and went on to be an All-Pro at two positions.

CHAPTER SEVEN

THE DAY GEORGE ANDRIE DIED

Lilly wasn't the only Cowboy who had an opinion on every subject. Ralph Neely griped about everything. He always had a better way of doing things. No matter what it was. His nickname was "Rotten." Ralph Rotten Neely. Because everything to Neely was rotten. The food was bad. We're eating too early. The beer wasn't cold enough. The sun was too hot. The wind was blowing too much. We weren't getting paid enough. He just bitched and moaned about everything. Everything was rotten.

Ralph was a good guy but he knew everything about everything. He was omniscient. There wasn't a subject that Ralph Neely didn't know something about. I told Ralph one time, "You know, Ralph, I finally figured you out. This is an age of specialists and that's what you are. A specialist is a guy who learns more and more about one subject. He learns more and more about less and less and pretty soon he's just like you. You know everything there is to know about nothing."

Charlie Waters and I were in our room whittlin one day

and Ralph comes in. Now Ralph never whittled in his life but he *knows*. Ralph is hanging over Charlie's shoulder and he's saying, "Now, Charlie, you need to do this and you need to do that." "No, no, you dummy, cut the end off first." On and on.

Finally Charlie's had enough and he turns around and looks at Ralph and says, "Ralph, I ain't like you. I wasn't born twenty-one. So there's a lot of things I don't know." And that stuck with Ralph the rest of his days with the Cowboys. That was Rotten. Rotten was the only guy born twenty-one. He never had to live and learn like the rest of us. He knew it all when he came screaming out of his mother's womb. Poor woman.

Ralph had these tapes he wanted us to listen to of the ocean with disguised subliminal messages. If we were gonna play in Green Bay and it was gonna be cold, the tapes would say something like, "You won't be cold. You won't be cold." Bullshit. When it's minus 10 degrees, it's cold. They could have you hypnotized colder than a marble statue and you'd still freeze your ass off in Green Bay in December.

D. D. Lewis told Ralph, "Why don't you sell those goddamn tapes and buy some good gloves cause, baby, you're gonna need em in Green Bay."

Rotten hasn't changed. He married a hypnotist and she hypnotized him into being skinny. When Charlie went to visit him he tried to convince Charlie this was the way to go. Charlie just shook his head. Once you're rotten, you're rotten to the core.

One thing Ralph definitely knew was how to play offensive tackle. He's probably the greatest offensive lineman the Cowboys ever had. He was a good one. If I had to run behind anyone I think I'd choose Ralph.

Ralph had as much physical talent as any offensive

lineman I've ever seen. He was huge and yet he had the agility and the hand and foot quickness that you need for pass protection. But he also had the strength to handle the running game.

Neely played the left side of the line, which is the toughest. First of all, it's the blind side of the quarterback. And, secondly, the pass protection on that side is like playing left-handed. Everything's backward. But Ralph stepped in from day one his rookie year and played great for the next twelve years.

Ralph went to Oklahoma University where he was a star and he ended up signing two pro contracts—one with the AFL's Houston Oilers and one with Dallas. This was right before the two leagues merged. So they had a big legal battle to see who'd get Neely. In the end, Dallas got to keep Rotten but part of the settlement was that we had to play the Oilers in three exhibition games at the Astrodome. They called the games the Ralph Neely Bowl.

It was just like Rotten to start a mess like that.

The only problem with Neely was he had a lot of injuries. He had three knee operations and a broken leg all in a five-year period. One year they drained his knee twenty-one times and the next year he played the entire season with a broken hand.

All Rotten's problems started the day George Andrie died.

A group of the Cowboys started riding motorcycles. On Mondays after the game, we'd usually go out to Grapevine Lake and ride out in the dirt all day. Mike Ditka was with the Cowboys then and he bought a 125cc. Dave Edwards had a 125. Me and Lilly and Cliff Harris and Reeves had one. And, of course, that meant Ralph had to have one too.

Rotten couldn't ride worth a damn. He kept falling off all day. But that didn't make any difference. His bike had to be bigger and better than everybody else's. So Ralph went out and bought a Husqvarna 400, an absolute man-eating monster. Comes with a chair and a whip.

Anyway, we'd been out riding all day and we're packing it up to go home and off in the distance I could see Cliff coming in and his eyes are as big as silver dollars. And I thought, "Oh, shit. What happened?"

Cliff and Rotten had been riding together and Ralph says, "Cliff, let's jump some hills."

And Cliff was thinking, "Christ, Ralph, you can barely ride. And now you want to jump hills?" Plus, he knew Ralph had a herd of ponies under him like to scare the shit outta Cochise. But he figured, "Ah, what the hell!"

There was a grass field out where they were riding and at the end of it was a hill that went up at a nice pitch. Nothing too scary. So Cliff gunned his 125 and went right up the hill and waited there for Ralph.

Ralph guns his monster and gets about halfway up and falls over. So he gets up cussing, "Damn motorcycle ain't worth a shit. They don't make nothing worth a damn anymore."

Good ol Rotten.

So Ralph goes back down and tries it again, only this time he really cranks that puppy up full throttle. Here comes Ralph *eeeeeeeeeee,* thumb, *eeeeeeeeeee,* thumb, *eeeeeeeeeee,* about 60 or 70 mph and he climbs right up to the top . . . and keeps right on going. He shoots into the air about twenty feet.

Ralph's legs are real long and instead of putting them on the footrest, he used to ride with them dangling along the ground. Well, he lands on his back and starts rolling down the hill with those big ol legs going every whichaway. When he finally stops he looks back up at Cliff and says real calmly, "Ah, Cliff, I think I hurt my foot. Look at it would you?"

And sure enough his leg was pointing up the hill and his foot was pointing down. He'd broken it in three places, dislocated his ankle and tore a bunch of ligaments. Out for the season.

They throw Rotten in the back of Ditka's truck with the muddy old bikes and every time they'd go over a bump Neely would scream. But nobody gave a damn about Neely's pain. All they kept saying to him all the way home was, "Don't tell Landry we were riding motorcycles. Let's tell him we were riding horses. Ya, we were riding along and a snake bit Ralph's horse."

So they take him over to the hospital and that night there was a team party. When I got there, somebody comes running up to me and says, "Did you hear what happened?"

"Hell, I was with him when it happened."

"You were there when George Andrie had his heart attack?"

"What? Andrie had a heart attack?"

"Ya."

"Didn't you hear about Neely?" I asked.

"No."

"He broke his leg."

"How'd he do it?"

"He stepped off a curb and it snapped."

"No shit."

Turned out Andrie never did have a heart attack. It was just indigestion. But it sure helped take Landry's mind off Neely's foot and how he did it. The funny thing was there were seven of us Cowboys all happy as hell that George was dying of heart failure. Just as long as Landry didn't find out we'd been riding motorcycles.

Who says you don't get close with your teammates?

CHAPTER EIGHT

THE BEST LITTLE WHITTLER IN TEXAS

Reeves and I had the "recreation room." Our room was the place where everybody gathered in training camp or before a game. I'd just love to have people come by and we'd sit around and drink beer and bullshit and I'd whittle.

Whittlin is relaxin. I started whittlin when I first played with the Cowboys because, believe it or not, it helped me gain weight. The trainers were always trying to keep my weight up. At the time I was trying to maintain 195 to 200 pounds but I couldn't do it.

When I graduated from high school I weighed 160 pounds. And I didn't grow until my freshman year at OSU when I started eating regular. They had a training table up there and I just stuffed myself everyday. I was also doing a little training at Milly's Bar and Grill. When I came back for Thanksgiving my freshman year I weighed 210. That's the most I've ever weighed in my life before or since.

But with the Cowboys I usually played at 187. I played one year at 178! Now that's all right if you're Bullet Bob

Hayes. But when you're Slow As Shit Garrison that don't cut it.

Every year I'd show up at training camp at 205 and in a week I'd be down to 195 and dropping fast. I did everything to keep my weight up. They gave me these supplements—some weird concoctions with molasses in it. Tasted like old socks. Never gained an ounce. My metabolism was like a hummingbird's. I'd eat like a mudhog and I'd lose weight.

Finally they said, "What you need to do is go home, sit down, drink a beer and relax. And then eat. Don't go home and eat right away because you're so keyed up your system burns it all up."

So I tried to go home and relax. But I really couldn't do it till I started whittlin. I'd go home and I was liable to sit there for an hour and a half or two hours whittlin and drinking three or four beers. And then I'd eat and it helped me maintain my weight.

At training camp I used to whittle all the time. I'm not a guy who can take a nap during the day. I still can't. A lot of guys could come in after the first practice of the day and sleep two or three hours, then get up and go practice again. But I had to be doing something. So I'd sit there and whittle, dip a little snuff and whittle some more. And the whole time guys would be comin by and we'd bullshit for a while.

I've made all sorts of things over the years, from wooden chains to old cowboys in their underbritches to flowers. In fact, one of my pieces is famous now. But nobody knows it. Except me and Burt Reynolds.

I met Burt way back in 1966. Me and Reeves and Meredith and Dial went to a party at Ryan O'Neal's house when he was still married to Ali MacGraw. I was rooming with Reeves back then and that meant I got in on a lot of things most other rookies didn't get in on. Reeves was on the "A" list as far as social events went cause him and Meredith hung out together and Don was the social director of the Cowboys.

Meredith comes by our room one night and says, "OK, Frog, let's go. And you, ya, you. What's your name? Ya, you can come too."

So we get to the party and we walk in and O'Neal kind of announces us, "Hey, it's Don Meredith and Dan Reeves and Buddy Dial and, aaaaaah . . ." When he gets to me he's stumped, so he whispers, "Ah, what's your name?"

"Walt Garrison."

"And Walt Harrison."

So I'm kinda pushed over into the corner and, of course, Meredith is the life of the party. They're all drinking and bullshittin with all these Hollywood bigshots. And I end up sitting on the couch next to some guy.

"Hi, I'm Walt Garrison."

"Hi, I'm Burt Reynolds."

Eventually I got around to asking him what he did. "I'm a stunt man in Hollywood. I got a break the other day. I'm Marlon Brando's double in his new movie, *One-Eyed Jacks.*"

He'd also played the blacksmith on *Gunsmoke* but nobody knows who he is. So, anyway, we get to visitin and we been friends ever since.

I was in Bishop, out in the California desert, doing a commercial for Dodge trucks one time and on my way back through L.A., I decided to go see Burt.

I call him up and I say, "I'm gonna stop on over."

"Good," he says.

When I got to L.A. I called and his bodyguard answered and said. "Boss wants you to meet him at the studio. Stage 45."

So I head over there and walk in this huge studio and there's nobody in there and I kinda wander around and, finally, I see someone way over in the corner. Turns out to be Burt and Dolly Parton. They're rehearsing for *The Best Little Whorehouse in Texas.*

I sat around and watched for a while and like I say I

ain't much good at sitting doing nothing. So I found an old broomstick handle and I start to whittlin on it while Burt and Dolly are jacking around rehearsing. And when they get done, they come on over and Burt says, "Hey, that's a good idea."

"What?"

"The whittling. I need to be whittling on something in this opening scene. But I need it to look like something. Not just like I'm making a long stick shorter. Can you whittle me something?"

"Sure. Whadda ya want?"

"I don't know. But I need it so people can see it's something. Not just me carving a stick."

"OK. How about a chain?"

"Oh, ya, a chain would be great."

Well, I got me a piece of oak so he wouldn't break it and I whittled him about five links of a chain. But I didn't finish it. Just left it dangling from the piece of wood it was carved outta. So it looks like he's still working on it.

So in the opening scene of *The Best Little Whorehouse in Texas* there's Burt whittlin on this chain. That's my chain!

Burt's been a friend of mine through the years. He was a friend of mine when nobody knew who the hell Burt Reynolds was. We were buddies and then, all of a sudden, he's a big star. But just because he hit it big, he wasn't the type who pretended he didn't know you anymore.

I took my first wife Pam out to the studio one time to meet Burt and Pam's afraid he's gonna be a big snob. And I told her, "No, no. He's a great guy. You're gonna love him."

So we show up and Burt comes in and I mean he is friendly as hell to Pam, "Hi, how are ya. Nice to meet you." And he gets his arm around her and off they go to see the set. She ended up thinking he was the greatest guy in the world.

Hey, tell you the truth, he is.

I feel sorry for Burt though. We went out one night to

eat and Burt couldn't even go because he'd get mobbed. He said, "I wouldn't have a good time and neither would you."

So he stayed home. Damn shame though. Like Meredith said, "We had eight hundred dollars' worth of fun that night."

Brother Harv is the one who got me interested in whittlin. Walter Harvey's his real name but he used to buy these old churches and make them into barbecue joints, so they called him Brother Harv. He bought one old church out by the Texas stadium, painted it red, fixed it up inside and called it "Harvey's."

He's got the place decorated up and there's signs hanging on all the walls. Stuff like:

"Illiterate: Write here for free help."

"Etc.: Something you use to make people think you know more than you do."

"Doing good is no fun unless you're caught in the act."

"This country would be better off if we had more whittlers and less chiselers."

Harv's got his whittlin all over the place. It's helped his business. A lot of people would come by Harvey's just to see his whittlin. Actually, Brother Harv is a wood carver. If you're real good at whittlin, you're a wood carver. If you're just making shavings or a chain that ain't worth a shit, then that's whittlin.

I used to go over there and eat barbecue and whittle just to see what I could pick up from the old master. But the darn guy never would tell me anything. I'd ask him, "Hey, Harvey, would you sell me this chain, so I can go home and copy it?"

And he'd say, "No."

"Well, why not, fer Christ's sake?"

"If I sell you that, Walt," he'd say, "then there wouldn't be nothin there. And we need something in that space on the wall."

He wouldn't tell you any of his secrets about whittlin. But one time I got hurt. I had a pinched nerve in my neck and I couldn't practice for two or three weeks and I didn't have nothing to do. So I'd go on over to Brother Harv's every day and whittle with him. He's got a little bench in there and I was sitting there whittlin a chain and finally he said, "Let me show you something."

And he took a table saw and he cut out this cross in the wood. "Now," he said, "whittle a chain outta that."

I said, "Harv, why didn't you tell me that about five or six months ago?"

"Walt, if I took the time to help everyone who comes in here who wants to whittle, I'd never get anything done. Lots of people see my whittlin around here and they *think* they want to whittle. But they don't want to spend the time it takes to make anything. But it looks like you're gonna stick with it, so I'm gonna show you some stuff."

And it's been a real close friendship ever since.

I taught a few of the Cowboys to whittle. Charlie Waters took it up and he was gonna whittle him a whole freakin chess set. That was his big goal. He whittled for a month in training camp and ended up with one little ol horse that looked like a gay goat.

Bob Lilly took it up and he learned to whittle pretty good. He got to where he could actually make something. But Lilly's the artist type anyway.

The problem with teaching guys how to whittle is it can get dangerous, especially if you ever have to use your fingers again. I gave Charlie a knife to whittle with that was just sorta sharp, so he couldn't really do much damage to himself. It'd cut wood but it wasn't really lethal. One day we were whittlin and I went to take a leak and Charlie thought he'd see what one of my knives was like. So he reached over to my bed and got one of the knives that was sittin there. But this baby was *sharp*. And he went to take a slice outta his piece of wood and it went through it like warm lard and kept right on going through his finger. He cut the hell out of it.

They fixed him up and Landry told me, "Hey, take those knives away from Charlie before he takes a couple of fingers off." So that was the end of Charlie's chess set.

Ralph Neely whittled for a while and he cut a bunch of his fingers. He said, "Shit, I'm gonna have to stop whittling or I won't be able to hold on the pass rush anymore."

Neely was famous for holding. He got caught holding more than a whore during Mardi Gras. I got a picture of Neely hanging in my office that Neely sent me of him holding defensive end Dave Rowe from St. Louis. Rotten's got Dave's jersey all wrapped up in both hands so the guy could barely move. "To Walt," it says, "Keep on holding on."

Then there was the night the teacher got taught.

It was all Lilly's fault. One time before a game Bob brought in a hunting knife for me to sharpen. So I put a hell of an edge on that puppy. Then I decided I'd whittle a little bit. I had a block of wood I carried with me and a couple pocket knives. I wanted to cut a chunk off that block, so I thought, "Man, Lilly's knife looks ideal." Only thing was, it was so sharp it went right through that wood and cut my index finger down to the bone. The whole finger was just hanging there. Blood was gushing out all over the place. It was making such a mess, I had to pull a wastebasket over and let it bleed in there. And I like to fill the damn basket up.

Charlie Waters was rooming with me then and he threw up, freaked out and fainted all at the same time. Then he started screaming, "Walt, you cut your finger off! You cut your finger off!"

Charlie called down for the team doctor but, of course, he was out eatin. So I told Charlie to go down to the trainers' room and get me some tape while I held my finger together. A few minutes later Charlie came back with the tape and I taped the finger back on. Then I got a big bucket of ice and stuck my finger in it and went to sleep.

Only Charlie couldn't sleep a wink all night. "You pissed me off so bad that night," he said. "You were sound asleep with your hand in that bucket of ice and I stayed up all night. I thought you were gonna bleed to death, so I kept checking to see if the ice bucket was filling up with blood."

The next morning I went out to the stadium and the doctor sewed me up. He put nineteen stitches in my finger right before the game. And I told him, "Don't tell Tom."

"OK, but just don't fumble."

I ended up having a great day. I caught seven passes, one of them in the end zone for a TD, and gained 120 yards on the ground. And Charlie played the worst game of his career.

And all because I needed something to relax.

Of course, in recent years, quite a few people have been using drugs to relax.

I was real naive about drugs when I first joined the Cowboys. It wasn't like now, where kids are on a first-name basis with their local pharmacist when they're in junior high. Hell, I was shocked when I saw Meredith smoking a cigarette at halftime my first exhibition game.

That game was a real learning experience for me. After the game they had a buffet set up in the dining hall. And I looked over there and there's a big stack of beer. And I'm thinking, "That must be for the coaches and press." Just then Lilly and Andrie walk in, grab a tray and walk right on past all the food, load three six packs apiece on their trays and go on over and sit down and start drinking.

Pro football players drinking beer in front of the coaches! I was shocked.

Before that game I was sitting in the locker room and somebody came around with a shoe box filled with little envelopes like the flower shops give you. And each envelope had the name of a player on it.

He would start at one end of the locker room and he'd come up to each player and he'd look through the box for the guy's envelope. Then he'd give it to him and he'd go to the next guy. He gave Howley an envelope, Perkins got one, Edwards, Jordan—right on down the line. Just about everyone got one except me.

I didn't know what the hell it was. This went on for several weeks. So one time I asked Perkins, "What the hell is he passing out?"

"Oh, nothing," he says. "Just these little ol green hearts."

As stupid as I was, I still didn't know what the hell they were. "Oh, green hearts, great. What the hell are green hearts?"

"Makes your heart beat faster. Gives you a little more energy."

"Well, goddamn," I thought. "Perkins is taking them and he's starting. There must be something to it, cause I ain't taking them and my ass is on the bench."

So I got Reeves to get me a couple of them and I took them at practice one day. Now nobody took them at practice. But I figured when you took drugs, you'd just go off into another world. They'd find you on top of a building somewhere gone crazy.

I wanted to test them first in practice just in case I went nuts and O.D.'d on the sonuvabitches. They'd think I was sick or something. So I took them a couple times in practice and I couldn't tell that much difference other than I felt pretty good. And I could thread a sewing machine while it was going full tilt.

So I started taking them and I took them right up to the time I retired. Nobody ever suggested they were bad for you. Heck, your wife was taking them to lose weight.

Finally, under pressure, the NFL came down on them

in my fifth or sixth year in the league. They did away with everything. They couldn't give you anything stronger than an aspirin without a prescription.

So that meant we had to go to the black market. And, believe me, that was probably easier than getting them in the locker room. Hell, you could get them at any truck stop across the country. It's my firm belief that if a guy really wants to take any kind of drug, he can find it.

The prevalence of drugs in our society and among sports figures started during the late sixties and early seventies among young people, mostly of college age who lived through that hippie, counterculture, social revolution that was going on back then.

Marijuana smoking got popular among football players just about the time I was retiring because that's about when all those kids who went to college during that drug-oriented time were starting to fill up the pro football teams.

Prior to that almost no one smoked pot. After that, almost everyone did. That's the way people are. They tend to do what everybody else is doing. Why would a guy be any different just because he's a football player?

There were some guys I knew on the team who smoked marijuana, but not many. Nobody got together and said, "Come on over to the house and we'll have a pot party."

There wasn't any cocaine around when I was playing. And I never heard about anybody using it. Cocaine as a widespread drug in our society appeared later. I guess my attitude about cocaine was summed up by a cowboy named Kenny Davis.

"First off," he said, "ain't nothin goin up my nose but my finger. Second, a hundred dollars for a couple of ground-up aspirin? In Abilene, Texas, for a hundred bucks, you can get a room at the Ramada Inn, a case of cold Pearl Lite and a hooker with kneepads."

CHAPTER NINE

THE VARMINT BROTHERS

If I was ever bored with the Cowboys, the boredom stopped the day Don Talbert joined the team. I remember the day we acquired Talbert. Charlie came up to me and said, "Oh, man, Walt, we are gonna have us a gooooood time now."

Talbert was without a doubt the wildest sonuvabitch ever to put on a uniform. Unless, of course, you count his brother Diron who played for the Rams. They also had a brother Charlie who was wilder than both of them. He was an All-American at Texas like Don but he never played pro ball. He's an accountant.

Talbert had actually played for the Cowboys before. In 1962 he got drafted out of Texas University and spent the year with Dallas. Then he got drafted by Uncle Sam and spent the next two years in Saigon as a military policeman. He came back to the Cowboys in 1965. They traded him the next year and he played for several teams. Then we got him back in 1971.

Lucky us.

We went hunting out to Sulphur Springs one time and Toni Fritsch was shooting meadowlarks and all kinds of field birds. Hell, Toni don't know any better. He was a city boy. He thought they were geese. And Talbert said, "Look at that dumb son of a bitch killing those poor birds. Let's get him."

Fritsch was over by a corrugated tin lean-to sneaking up on this meadowlark and Talbert opens up on him. That was one of Talbert's favorite pastimes. He liked to scare you a little. He'd just aim a little high with a shotgun and let the buckshot sprinkle down all over you.

He got Edwards the same weekend. And Edwards looked at him and said, "Ah, Talbert, you goddamn varmint."

And after that they called Talbert "Varmint" and when he and his crazy brothers got together they were "The Varmint Brothers." And the name fit them like Christie Brinkley fits into a bathing suit. Those mothers was indecent.

About a dozen Cowboys lived in an apartment house called The Four Seasons. That's where the story *North Dallas Forty* actually took place. Anyway, the whole bunch of them decided to go dove hunting one day. So they all jumped in the back of a pickup. A guy from the apartment house named Sam Jones was driving. He was about seventy. Everybody called him "Raisin" cause he was all shriveled up.

Well, the hunting wasn't too good so they got to drinking "bird bigger." Talbert used to say, "If you have a dozen beers, instead of them son of a bitching birds looking like flies coming at you, they look like turkeys. And the more you drink, the bigger the birds get."

So they called all the booze they drank "bird bigger."

There were about twelve Cowboys in the back of this truck and they hadn't seen anything all day. But on the way back to town Talbert spots this damn dove sitting on a fence out by this old shack in the country and he starts blasting away. BOOM! BOOM! BOOM! And it wasn't just one shot. That varmint emptied his gun.

And there's this old guy in his overalls sittin in a swing on the front porch. He leaps up outta that swing and jumps in his pickup and chases us down the road. He's got ladders and paint buckets hanging off his truck. He comes roaring out of his driveway at about 60 mph, skids out onto the road in that paint truck with ladders swinging around and buckets flying all over the road. He finally pulls up alongside our truck and yells, "Pull over! Pull over!"

Lee Roy, who's in the back of the truck, leans over the cab and tells Sam Jones, "You better pull over or this son of a bitch is gonna shoot our tires out from under us."

So Raisin pulls over and this old farm boy jumps out of his truck and runs around to the back of our truck and yells, "Who's the asshole who was shooting back there at my house. You coulda killed my kids."

Lee Roy is trying to calm this guy down.

"Sir, we're sorry. We didn't mean to. We were just emptying our guns. We had a shell or two left and we were just getting rid of them. We're gonna be real nice. We're just gonna head on up the road."

So the guy says, "All right, I just don't like to hear no firing out around my house."

We all settle back down and Lee Roy tells Sam, "Go ahead." And we pull out and this guy goes to get back in his truck and Talbert yells, "Hey, you big loudmouthed bastard. It was me shootin at your kids."

Oh shit!

This guy jumps in his truck again and Jordan yells to Sam, "Raisin! Drive like hell!"

We take off and that sonuvabitch chases us again only this time we're almost in town. We're all doin 90 to 100 mph on a two-lane road and there's paint cans flying off his truck and one of his ladders comes loose and that goes crashing onto the highway. He finally gets in front of us and pulls us off the road again.

And this time he's really pissed. I'm thinking he's gonna kill us all. He comes back around to the back of the truck and he's yelling, "Where's that mouther? That son of a bitch that's talkin so big. Come out here, mouther. I'm gonna kick your ass."

And Lee Roy is pleading with this guy cause he can just see the headlines the next day.

"Now, sir, we don't need no problem. We need to get on back to town."

Finally he gets this guy calmed down again. So we got going again and we get about twenty feet and Talbert starts yelling, "You mealy bastard. You no good . . ."

And here comes this ol boy again. This time though we're in town and Lee Roy screams at Raisin, "Just keep on driving and don't stop for nothin." And, luckily, we finally lost the guy in traffic.

After that Varmint had himself another name—"The Mouther."

Varmint loved to hunt. We were playing the Redskins at Texas Stadium one time and Talbert took a vicious hit and twisted his ankle and he was limping around the rest of the game. But he played. After the game, Don and I and a friend of mine, Bill Robinson, went coon hunting. We got the coon dogs up and went out in the woods and Talbert was limping along after us. Bill and I were messing with him, kicking him in the ass, "Come on, you slow bitch."

We walked the creeks, up and down big hills and Talbert's back there hobbling along. Talbert was scared of snakes, so we'd throw sticks back at him and he'd jump. We walked fifteen or twenty miles following them dogs.

Who would have thought from these humble beginnings that I'd grow up to be so suave and debonair?

One of the Fightin Farmers of Lewisville High and the face that got voted "most handsome" in the senior class. Of course, there were only twenty-seven kids in the class so it wasn't exactly like getting picked Mr. Universe. (GEORGE HOLCOMB)

My first carry in pro ball I ran for sixty-five yards, and I probably would have scored if Bullet Bob Hayes (number 22) hadn't slowed me down. (©*DALLAS MORNING NEWS*, PHOTO BY ALECK PANTAZE)

My college coach, Phil Cutchin. He was a son of a bitch on the field, but afterward he turned out to be a nice guy. (BILL SLOAN)

This is the kind of hot-dog catch that gets headlines and a nice warm spot on Landry's bench. (©*DALLAS TIMES HERALD*, PHOTO BY JOHN MAZZIOTTA)

Three city slickers—Meredith, Reeves and Jordan—take the bull by the horns while I keep him steady. Lee Roy did all right, but that steer tossed Don and Dan around like a couple of rag dolls. (DAVE EDWARDS)

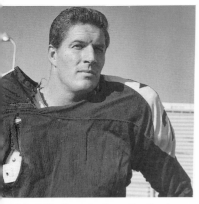

Mr. Lilly. Everybody on the Cowboys had a nickname except Bob Lilly. Bob was too big for anyone to start calling him names. (BOB LILLY)

Me, Billy Robinson and a couple of cold beers after a long day of bulldoggin. (DAVE EDWARDS)

Dan Reeves was the only running back in the NFL who was slower than I was. Staubach even had to tell him which way to run on this play. (© DALLAS TIMES HERALD. PHOTO BY JOHN MAZZIOTTA)

Life and football were one big party for Joe Don.
(BOB LILLY)

"Turn out the lights, the party's over..." (BOB LILLY)

Charlie Daniels (left) ain't just a good singer, he can ride too. Me and Charlie defeated Buddy Pauley and Larry Mahan in a team ropin' contest up at the Eastern Montana Fairgrounds. (MILES CITY STAR)

The only known picture of Tom Landry smiling. (BILL SLOAN)

More than one Cowboy lost his shorts playing cards. (BOB LILLY)

Below left: Little Puddin'
(BOB LILLY)

Below right: Staubach was the kind of guy if you did a thousand push-ups he'd do a thousand and one.
(BOB LILLY)

I sounded like Pee Wee
Herman after this play.
(©DALLAS TIMES HERALD.
PHOTO BY JOHN RHODES)

Varmint and me.
(AUTHOR'S COLLECTION)

Sports Illustrated

SEPTEMBER 18, 1972   60 CENTS

DALLAS SCRAMBLES TO STAY ON TOP

COWBOY WALT GARRISON

PRO FOOTBALL

After we won the Super Bowl they put me on the cover of *Sports Illustrated*.
(© *SPORTS ILLUSTRATED*)

Hall of Famer Mike Ditka had the worst temper of any man I ever met. (BOB LILLY)

Making commercials is nothing but fun.
(U.S. TOBACCO CO.)

"Just a pinch…"
—the words that made me famous.
(BILL SLOAN)

Debbie and I live abo
our new barn just up
the road from
Lewisville. (BILL SLOAN)

The next day Talbert's in the training room and he says, "Boy, my ankle is sore. I musta twisted it bad."

So he goes over and gets it X-rayed and he'd just shattered it. The ankle was broken in five places.

And Bill and I had made him walk twenty miles, jackassing him the whole way. "Come on, you wimp. There's nothing wrong with your ankle."

Did I mention that besides being a little wild, Talbert was tough!

I was at a rodeo in Austin once and Talbert shows up. Don was dropping by to take us over to a bar he owned in town. Well, anyway, they got this FFA Fair going and there's a bunch of hogs in this pen. And one of them hogs is making an awful noise, *ggggggggrrrrrrrr, eeeeeeeeeeee.* And Talbert reaches over the pen and blam! he hits this pig on the snout and knocks it out cold.

This little girl starts screaming, "Oh, God, he killed my pig. He killed my pig."

Well, a cop shows up. "What the hell did you hit the pig for?" he wants to know.

And Talbert says, "The mother was way outta line."

And the cop just shrugged. He figured he didn't need to deal with a 280-pound maniac who punches out pigs because they're "outta line."

Talbert wasn't completely nuts though. He knew when he was in a fight he couldn't win. Talbert had a girl from Dallas and a girlfriend from Austin and one night he's in this bar with his Austin honey, and his girl from Dallas surprises him and comes in. And Talbert sees her and jumps up and gets behind the bar. And me and Bill say, "What're you gonna do, Varmint?"

"The hell with em," he says. "Let em fight it out."

I was up in Colorado at a rodeo one summer and Don and his brother Diron, Myron Patios and Dave Elmendorf were in town. They all played for the Rams at the time and they were helping out teammate Roman Gabriel who had a football camp up there. We all went out to eat one night at this little Mexican joint. The mayor and the president of the Chamber of Commerce and a bunch of civic leaders set it up and it was a big deal. They had a mariachi band in there playing with a couple of Spanish dancers. Real nice little group. But Talbert listened to them for about five minutes then he gets up on the stage and says, "OK, y'all are done. Get the hell outta here and sit down. We brought our own entertainment."

Jerry Lane was a friend of mine, a Country and Western singer/song writer. His big hit was "Asphalt, It's Your Fault." Jerry had come along for the ride up there, so he was with us that night.

"OK, come on up here and sing, Lane."

Then Talbert sat by the door and he wouldn't let anybody in the place. He kidnapped the restaurant. Somebody'd come through the door and he'd say, "Get out!" And they'd take one look at Talbert and they'd git. Every once in a while he'd let one of them in. If she was good-lookin mostly. Then he'd say, "Now sit down and shut up."

A quiet little guy came in with snow-white hair and a cute little suit and Talbert says, "Sit right here." And the guy sits down and Talbert jerked the tablecloth off the table and threw it around this guy's neck and says, "Well, while I gotcha here, I thought I'd just cut your hair." And the guy went berserk and ran outta there.

Well, as the night went on, somebody's wife got half drunk and she was flirting with just about everyone. Just pissed her husband off bad. Eventually she took a shine to Varmint. (I told you she was drunk.) Anyway, she thought she was gonna have some fun with Talbert, so she took the tablecloth and put it around Talbert and said, "While I gotcha here, I thought I'd just cut your hair."

And Talbert reached behind him and pulled her over his shoulder and laid her across his lap and said, "While I gotcha here, I think I'll just whup your ass."

And he did too. He spanked her good. And she was just a kickin and a hollerin. Meanwhile her husband was just laughing himself to death. He figured she needed it.

Mike Ditka and Dave Edwards owned a bar in Houston and I walked in there one night and there was Mike.

"How's it going, Mike?"

"Well, it's great," Ditka says. "But those Varmint Brothers come in last week. I told them just to drink what you want to and they just got drunker than hell. And they're slobbering and pinching the girls' asses and pullin their dresses over their heads. Shit like that.

"I'd have asked em to leave but I wouldn't know how. Finally, they get ready to go. And Don gets up on the stage with the band and there's slobber comin outta his mouth and he yells, 'Hey, turn that shit off. I got something to say.'

"So they turn the music off and Talbert screams, 'I'll see all you sonuvabitches later.'

"And finally they stumble outta the place."

And Ditka moans and says, "Ah, geez, now that's hard on business."

Ditka didn't have much luck with his friends in football. They were the main attraction of the place but they were also a big pain in the ass. I was there the night E. J. Holub, the behemoth linebacker for the Kansas City Chiefs, came in. Only problem was he came in on a horse. And it wasn't no Shetland pony either. Damn thing looked like a Clydesdale.

We were all in there after a game and we look up and here comes E.J. on his trusty steed right through the front doors of Ditka's place and down the stairs and backed that baby right up in the corner and yelled, "Y'all get my horse some beer."

And he sat on that horse for an hour just sipping beer and bullshittin. Then he rode on outta there the same way he come in. And there was poor ol Ditka in the back of the bar with this sorry-ass look on his face watching his investment go to hell.

"Ah, geez, now that's hard on business."

Every dog has his day though. Talbert's calmed down quite a bit since he retired. He's a businessman now. Don and his brothers owned about eight Holiday Inns in this area last time I heard. So he's doin real good. And I guess all that money makes you respectable.

After the Varmint Brothers put in the Holiday West in Houston, I was in town one day and I had a little time to kill so I said, "Hell, Talbert's over to the Holiday Inn, I'll just go over there and see him."

Well, I was already half gassed when I got there.

"Is Don Talbert in?"

"*Mister* Talbert has gone to the Chamber of Commerce meeting. He'll be back shortly. If you'd care to wait in the lounge?"

Now I'd heard Varmint called a lot of things over the years but Mr. Talbert wasn't one of them.

I said, "Great. Tell that no good son of a bitch I'll be in the bar."

"All right, sir."

I go in the bar and I start running a tab and I tell the bartender, "Put this on Don Talbert's bill."

So I'm in there drinking for quite a while and, finally, here comes the Varmint himself and he's got on a three-piece suit and a preppy tie. So I scream at the top of my lungs, "HEY, YOU SONUVABITCH! HOW YOU BEEN?"

Talbert says, "Oh, geez, Walt. Don't say that."

So I yell, "WELL, SIT ON DOWN HERE AND I'LL BUY YOU A GODDAMN DRINK!"

"All right," he whispers, "but heck, Walt, these people don't know me like you do."

"UP YOURS, VARMINT! GET UP HERE AND GET YOU A DRINK!"

I'd been in there for four hours embarrassing the shit outta him, cussin real loud and telling everyone what a gooooood friend Talbert was of mine.

Turns out Varmint don't even drink anymore. So I stayed there a couple more hours drinking his booze and embarrassing him, telling everyone all these stories about Talbert and what an asshole he used to be and how I don't believe he's changed a bit.

And the whole time I kept thinking about what Ditka said when the Varmint Brothers used to go in *his* bar and run everybody outta there.

"Ah, geez, now that's hard on business."

Well, I got Talbert's ass good that day. And all I can say is, "This butt's for you, Ditka."

CHAPTER TEN

THE KICKING KARAVAN

For some reason the Cowboys have always had a hell of a time finding a kicker. So one year Gil Brandt gets this idea that he and an entourage from the Cowboy front office are going to barnstorm the country in search of a kicker. They called it "The Cowboy Kicking Karavan" and the idea was to stop in various cities and towns across the USA and hold tryouts for prospective kickers. The damn thing stopped in twenty-nine cities from Oregon to New Jersey, covered twelve thousand miles and auditioned over thirteen thousand hopefuls. Everyone and anyone was invited out to try to kick his way into the NFL. It was a real Cinderella story.

In Memphis, a city bus pulled up alongside the field where the Kicking Karavan was in session. The driver hops off the bus and runs out onto the field in his gray uniform and black work shoes with his money changer still hanging on his belt. He hands the money changer to one of the coaches, kicks three balls off the side of his foot, says, "Much obliged for the tryout." And runs back to his bus while his passengers cheer him.

In Columbia, South Carolina, a kid kicked half a dozen punts about 20 or 25 yards and looked at Brandt and said, "Y'all signing any holders?"

This fiasco included Ermal Allen, the backfield coach; Ben Agajanian, the kicking coach; trainer Larry Gardner; Brandt's assistant, Norm Smith; an advance publicity man, Paul Manassah; a revolving door of assistants and, of course, Brandt himself. The whole bunch of them were chauffeured around in a chartered plane by a chartered pilot. It ended up costing the Cowboys a real bundle.

Tex Schramm would never reveal the real cost of this turkey but Danny Villanueva, at the time the resident kicker for the Cowboys, had a guess.

"I know what happened. Brandt was sitting up there in his office one afternoon and he thought, 'Somewhere in this great, big beautiful country of ours there has to be a better kicker than Villanueva.' So he blew $70,000 trying to find him."

They kept telling Danny and everyone else that this project was not launched because they were dissatisfied with Villanueva's performance. Ya, sure.

When it was all over the Cowboys invited ten kickers to come to training camp. They ended up signing two—Harold Deters of North Carolina State and Mac Percival, a twenty-seven-year-old former Texas Tech basketball star. They kept Deters and traded Percival to the Bears and he ended up being a pretty good kicker for Chicago. Deters was gone within a month, back teaching school in Dallas where he belonged.

In the end, all the Cowboys succeeded in doing was getting a pretty good kicker for Chicago. So it was back to the drawing board and Villanueva.

When the Cowboys couldn't find a kicker anywhere in America, they tried other continents. Colin Ridgway was a kicker from Lamar Tech by way of Australia. He was an

Olympic high jumper who'd cleared 7′1″. He could drop kick the ball through the goal posts from 50 yards 80 percent of the time and punt the ball 60 to 80 yards. Now here was the kicker of Landry's dreams.

But Villanueva knew how to handle everything the Cowboys threw at him. In preseason Danny and Colin were battling for the kicking position when Dallas played a game against the 49ers in Kezar Stadium where the strength of the wind is legendary.

Danny was on the headphones when the call came down from the coaches to get in there and punt. The two punters had been alternating punts but Danny weren't no dummy. The Cowboys were kicking out of their own end zone against a 50 mph hurricane and no matter how well he kicked it, Villanueva knew the damn thing was going to look like a stone. So he goes over to Ridgway and tells him the coaches want him in there. And out on the field trots Colin like a lamb to the slaughter.

They snap the ball and Ridgway really gets into this one sending it high and . . . Wait a minute! The damn thing gets caught up in the wind just like Villanueva knew it would and it starts coming back. Ridgway, who speaks this perfect King's English, looks up and says, "Blimey! It's coming back!"

Yep. And when the damn thing finally landed it was good for a 1-yard punt. First and ten, 49ers on their own 3-yard line. After that we called Ridgway "Boomerang."

And just like that Villanueva had taken care of another threat to his job.

The Cowboys finally got rid of Villanueva but they were still searching far and wide for kickers. This time Tex Schramm gets the idea that the best kickers are all over in Europe playing on the soccer teams. So he hires Bob Kap, a coach for the Dallas Tornados of the North American Soccer League, and sends him to Europe to sign a kicker.

Eventually Gil Brandt, Ermal Allen, Tom Landry and a few others flew over to Europe to look at the kickers Kap dug up. This little party ended up costing the Cowboys another thirty grand.

But at least this time they got somebody who could kick—Toni Fritsch. Fritsch was the star of the Austrian national soccer team who had beaten the world champion English team on their home field thanks to two goals by Fritsch. Toni was a national hero.

But apparently to Fritsch money spoke louder than glory. Fritsch had a tryout at Vienna Stadium and kicked 29 out of 30 field goals from the 40-yard line and the Cowboys signed him on the spot to a $15,000 guaranteed contract.

Toni Fritsch could kick all right but there were a few problems. First off, Toni couldn't speak a word of English when he joined the team. And who do you suppose volunteered to be his English tutor? None other than Professor Varmint himself. The first thing Talbert tells Fritsch is that the guy in the striped shirt is known as asshole. So in the first exhibition game of the season, Fritsch comes out to kick off and the referee hands him the ball and Toni says, "Thank you veddy much, Meester Asshole."

"Huh?"

"Thank you, asshole."

"Get this jerk outta here."

Then Talbert tells Toni that "goddamn" means "good morning." And, of course, that's the first thing Toni says to Landry.

"Goddamn, Coach Landry."

"What?"

"Goddamn, Coach."

And Landry looks around and says, "Where's Talbert?"

Toni's first roommate was Dan Reeves, a native Georgian. And the language gap was like the Grand Canyon. Reeves would come in after the coaches' meeting and Fritsch would be asleep in Dan's bed.

Reeves kept trying to explain whose bed was whose.

"Toni, this over here is Toni's bed. And this is Dan's bed, *verstehen*?" Reeves had picked up a little German from Ernie Stautner, the line coach who was a native of Bavaria, and he tried to sprinkle it in his conversation with Toni.

And Toni would wag his head in agreement with a big grin on his face. "Ya, ya. Goot bed, goot bed." And he'd lie back down in Dan's bed.

"Goddamnit Toni, this is *my* bed. This bed over here is Toni's bed."

And Toni'd smile.

"I know what the damn trouble is," Reeves said. "Fritsch has to figure out three languages. First he's gotta translate my crackerbarrel Georgian into English and then he's gotta translate *that* into German."

Reeves went to Stautner for help, so Ernie went and talked to Toni and when he came back he told Reeves, "Dan, I think you better just sleep in the empty bed."

The first day Fritsch came out for practice we'd all heard we had an Austrian kicker who couldn't speak English. It's the end of practice and we're gonna practice kick-offs. And Toni'd boot it impressively downfield and we'd all run down on coverage. Smooth as ice.

Then Tom says, "Now we're going to practice on-side kicks."

So we line up and we shift into the on-side kick formation and BOOM! Toni kicks it out of the end zone.

"No, no, no. On-side kick, Toni, on-side kick." We all line up again and BOOM! Into the end zone.

So, finally, Stautner walks up to Fritsch and puts his

hands on his shoulders and says real loud right into Toni's face, *"Ooon-siiiide keeeeeeek!"* Like that was gonna make a difference. So we line up and, sure enough, BOOM! Into the end zone it goes.

The whole team's gotta line up again and the rookies who are busting their asses trying to make the team don't know whether to run all the way down the field or what. Every time Toni kicks, half the team runs 50 yards downfield wasting all sorts of time which, of course, just delights Landry.

So Tom gets into it, "No, Toni, Ooooon-siiiiide keeeeek! Ooooon-siiiiiiide keeeeek!"

BOOM! Into the end zone.

Cliff Harris and Pat Toomay had a refrigerator in their room and they kept beer in there. They'd drink two or three beers a day and they'd be buying two or three *cases* a day because everybody would raid their fridge. Finally they put a cup on top of the fridge with a sign next to it that said, "If you take a beer, put some damn money in the cup."

Cliff and Pat would be trying to sleep and all night long the door would open and there would be Fritsch sneaking in to get him a beer. Ten minutes later the door would open and Toni was back for another beer. The night they put the cup up, Fritsch is back as usual. Toomay's watching him outta one eye and this time Toni notices the cup up there and, of course, he couldn't read the sign. So he reaches up there and, "Hey, what's this? Change!" And he puts it in his pocket and moseys on out again.

Pat just shook his head and went back to sleep. He'd already seen Landry try to explain an on-side kick. He was damned if he was gonna get into high finance with Fritsch.

Fritsch came from Germany where beer drinkin is serious business and he could really pack away the suds. Fritsch and Reeves had a TV in their room and every morning at seven or seven-thirty Fritsch would be in there drinking one of those 24-ounce Coors Tallboys. Out of Toomay's fridge, of course. He'd watch TV most of the morning and he couldn't understand a word of it. But it didn't seem to matter. Then he'd go down, get a sandwich and another beer, come on back and sit down in front of the TV. And that's what he did for training camp.

He thought he'd died and gone to heaven. He was getting paid more than he was in Germany to play soccer. Plus, over there he had to run up and down the field all day long. Worked him like a sled dog. In America he drinks all day and gets paid for it.

What a country!

During the regular season Toni's schedule was about the same. After the morning meeting everybody would go to the practice field. All except the kickers who were free to do whatever they wanted until the late afternoon when we'd run the kicking drills. Most of the kickers would do a little running, a little kicking, pump in the weight room for a while. At least put on a good show. Not Fritsch. He'd head straight over to a bar across from the stadium, The VIP, and drink.

Toward the end of practice, Toni'd come back for the special teams' drills and by then, of course, he was in the bag.

Fritsch never took football real serious. He thought it was sorta dumb. The same way most Americans thought soccer was sorta dumb back then. Of course, Landry was dead serious about football and it was inevitable they would clash.

We were gonna play Cleveland once and it was raining like hell in Cleveland so Landry gets this idea he's gonna make a mudhole out there so Fritsch could get practice kicking in the mud. And Fritsch takes one kick and says he's pulled a muscle or something and trots off the field.

Tom tells him to report to the trainers' room and the trainers tell him to ice his leg down and then get in the diathermy and follow a bunch of other therapy. And Fritsch listens for a while and then says, "No, I take three days off." And walks out and heads for The VIP.

The next week we were out on the practice field and The Big Cat, Rayfield Wright, was standing over on the sidelines and he says to me, "Check out Tom."

Landry's standing about ten feet away from Fritsch only Toni don't know it and Toni says, "Watch this. I going to keek. I tell them all to get back, get back and I go to keek the ball and I go Boop!"

Fritsch as usual was drunk as hell out there and he'd run up to kick the ball and he'd bang his toe on the ground about a foot in front of the ball and, sure enough, just like he said, the ball went Boop! We couldn't believe it.

Landry was pissed. He was standing there and he heard every damn word and we all knew Fritsch was going to be in trouble the next day at meetings.

Sure enough, Landry jumps all over Fritsch, "Toni, we take this game very serious here. When we practice we give it our all . . ." And Landry is going on and on and it looks like he's getting through to Fritsch. And finally Toni stands up and clicks his heels and yells, "Heil Hitler!"

Landry blew an everlovin gasket.

CHAPTER ELEVEN

THE ZERO CLUB

While the Cowboys were combing foreign shores for players, some wise guy at NFL films was making up a name for the Cowboys—"America's Team" which went over like a lead sinker in every town in America except Dallas.

But maybe we were America's Team. Dallas had the number-one TV ratings in pro football and we seemed to be on the tube every week. We had Dandy Don, the playboy quarterback, and Bullet Bob Hayes, the fastest human on earth. We had a high-powered offense that led the league in scoring and a high-tech stadium. And we won a lot. Plus, we had the best-looking cheerleaders.

But all that name ever brought us was grief. Everybody was out to get us. You'd go into a town and there'd be X-rated signs all over about America's Team. The Oilers beat us one year and after the game Bum Phillips said, "Well, they might be America's team but the Oilers are Texas's team."

The problem was Dallas *was* the most glamorous team in the league. We were showered with publicity and endorsements. And out of all this media hype it seemed inevitable that an institution like the "Zero Club" would emerge.

The Zero Club was made up of three guys on the Cowboys who nobody ever paid attention to—Larry Cole, Blaine Nye and Pat Toomay. They never got mentioned in the papers, nobody asked them to endorse their products, nobody interrupted their dinners to ask for an autograph and there sure wasn't a bunch of groupies trying to get them into the sack.

They were a bunch of zeroes.

The Zero Club was founded one night at training camp. We all had the night off and there's always a flurry of activity on a night like that. All the cool guys had nice clothes to wear, places to go and a car to go in. And by eight o'clock the dorm was a ghost town.

Toomay came outta his room and everybody was gone. He started drifting aimlessly down the hallway and he hears the sound of a TV somewhere. So he takes off in lukewarm pursuit and follows the sound down to the last room on the left. He looks in and there's Blaine Nye on the near bed staring up at the ceiling. On the far bed was Larry Cole sound asleep, snoring.

There was aluminum foil on the windows to block out the sun because it was summer and it wasn't dark out yet. But for all zeroes everywhere the day was over.

The TV was on all right but it was tuned to a test pattern and the vertical hold was shot, so the picture was rolling slowly over and over and there was static coming from the speaker. And Blaine Nye looked over at Toomay and said, "Welcome to the Zero Club."

And an institution was born.

Nobody in the Zero Club had a car, of course. But one night they decided to go to a movie together. So Pat called around to try to get a car and, of course, he couldn't. Finally they hitched a ride with a rookie and his girlfriend—which is the height of zero-ness. The rookie could get a car *and* a girl. But they couldn't get either.

The movie turned out to be *How to Frame a Fig* with Don Knotts. There was nobody at the theater but them. Afterward, the rookie was going to take his girl to dinner so he dumped them and they had to walk home.

All the members of the Zero Club agreed the evening had been a complete success.

The Zero Club was very exclusive. Nobody could get into it except for the three charter members because as soon as anybody showed any interest in joining, it proved they cared too much about something to be a zero. Larry Cole got his name in the paper once and Nye and Toomay put him on probation.

Larry Cole was a blond-haired defensive end who looked like Joe Palooka. He also grunted a lot like a caveman so they called him "Lurch."

Lurch had a very broad education. First he went to the Air Force Academy but he left because he wouldn't fink on a classmate who got caught cheating on exams. So he transferred to the University of Houston and spent a semester there. Then he went to the University of Hawaii.

When they got Cole up to sing his school song as a rookie in training camp, he sang "Tiny Bubbles," the song Don Ho sings to all the tourists. Cole thought it was a great song. Such things are zeroes made of.

Cole was from Granite Falls, Minnesota. All they do there is grow wheat and freeze to death. Larry was just a big ol farm boy. Toomay used to say, "Who else do you know who's got a tattoo on his arm that says, 'Born to Raise Wheat.'"

When Nye heard that his old club member was retiring, he sent a telegram that said, "I guess you could say Larry was my best friend for ten years. But when I think about our relationship today, I'd rather have had a dog."

In his final season Cole recovered a fumble against the Redskins and ran it back for a touchdown. It was his fourth touchdown in his career, all against the Redskins. But he hadn't had one in ten years. When a reporter asked him why it had taken him so long to get his fourth TD, Lurch said, "Hey, anybody can have an off decade."

The other two members of the Zero Club, Nye and Toomay, were both certifiable geniuses.

The entire nine years Nye was with the Cowboys he went to school at Stanford. He had a master's in physics but didn't like the job prospects of a theoretical physicist. So he went and got an MBA from Stanford which is the academic equivalent of gaining 2000 yards in a season.

Now he's a consultant. He figures actuarial stats. There's a plane or a car wreck and Nye figures out how much it will cost the company involved—before it happens. Don't ask me how he does it.

Talking with Nye was like talking to an encyclopedia. Here's this big dumb lineman who could come up with ideas that would make me dizzy and talk circles around me on any subject. He was brilliant.

Toomay was just as brilliant but he was more the artistic type. In other words, he was a weirdo. He ended up writing three or four books and a couple of screenplays.

Toomay was the kind who didn't fit in. He marched to a different drummer. He was one of those laid-back California types with long hair and a beard who your daddy warned you about.

Landry asked him one time, "Pat, when are you going to cut your hair?"

"As soon as I get back from Chicago, Coach."

"Good," Landry says, all encouraged because Toomay

was a pain in the ass to Landry. "When are you going to Chicago?"

"I ain't."

Toomay was way ahead of his time. He used to turn on the TV to the religious stations so he could harass all the TV evangelists. He was warning us about Tammy Faye's make-up fifteen years ago. Pat used to say, "How come when they tell you to send your money to Jesus, they give you their address?"

Toomay's nickname was "Ropes." If there was a short-cut, he'd find it. If there was a way to do it easier, he'd figure it out. He knew exactly when to come to practice. How long it took him to walk from the training room out to the practice field. And he would get there exactly at that time and not one second sooner.

He knew the ropes.

But poor Ropes was a victim of fate. He had bad karma piled up in his locker. Things were always happening to him he couldn't explain or control. He was a victim of the bizarre circumstances he always seemed to find himself in.

Fate just seemed to have it in for Pat. He had number-one draft choices lining up at his position every year to take his place. First it was Leroy Selman and then Tody Smith and he somehow survived both of them but not without a lot of grief and bench time.

But then the Cowboys took as their first draft pick Ed "Too Tall" Jones and nobody was gonna beat him out. In a matter of weeks, Toomay was gone.

Ropes always seemed to get roped with the worst room-mates.

For a while Pat got stuck rooming with Duane Thomas. Thomas ran up a big phone bill in Toomay's name. And the Cowboys got pissed at Pat because he got pissed at Thomas.

"Hey, I can't afford to room with Thomas anymore," he told them.

So then they stick him with Cliff Harris.

Cliff couldn't sleep the night before a game to save his butt and that meant Toomay got no sleep either. They gave Cliff three sleeping pills once and it didn't do a thing. Toomay was pissed. He was above all that. He could sleep anywhere, anytime. He played football—that was it. Emotion, nerves—they had nothing to do with the game. He couldn't understand why Cliff was so tense.

See, Pat was so laid back he had trouble getting up for a game at all. So the night before we played, he'd go out driving with Dave Edwards. Dave had a Porsche that would go 200 mph and he'd drive that thing as fast as he could through Dallas trying to scare the shit outta Toomay. And that would get Pat ready for the game.

"*Yaaaaaaaaaaaaoooooooooooooo!*" All over Dallas.

Cliff was another breed. He was hyped up, spaced out— a trigger lookin for a finger. So the trainers decided they'd give Cliff a huge sleeping pill. Had a nuclear warhead on it. And it knocked poor Cliff senseless. The problem was he still wasn't asleep. He was just crazy drunk. He was staggering all over the room, falling over chairs and Toomay had to stay up all night and take care of a drunkard. So he didn't get any sleep that night either.

Eventually Pat had the misfortune of being picked by the Tampa Bay Buccaneers in an expansion draft. And the Bucs promptly lost eighteen straight games. Maybe the worst team in pro football history. Finally Al Davis saves his life and gets Toomay traded to Oakland—a perennial winner. And who does Toomay get as a roomie—John Matuszak. The Tooz made Talbert look like an overachieving eagle scout.

The first time they room together Tooz comes in totally blitzed. He is 6'8" and 310 pounds. So he is a real bundle to handle even sober.

Now Ropes was famous for the way he dressed—or

rather didn't dress. If he had one decent clean shirt on the road he was black tie. So Toomay had this one good shirt with him and Tooz comes in stumbling and cussing—just really messed up. He looks like he's had a brawl with a garbage truck. His shirt is torn and his pants are all full of who knows what and his hair looks like he got it done at one of those fag salons in New York. Only afterward they sprinkled it with garbage.

So he rips off all his clothes and he spots Toomay's one good shirt and he says, "Hey, this is a pretty nice shirt." Before Toomay can say anything, he grabs it and puts it on and, of course, since he outweighs Toomay by 50 or 60 pounds he just rips the hell outta the shirt. The buttons all come flying off and the sleeves pop.

Then Matuszak stumbles out of the room wearing just Toomay's shirt, completely out of his mind running up and down the halls of this first-class hotel with everything hanging out.

Toomay figures he's just suffering some more of his damn bad roommate karma. So he shakes his head and calls downstairs for the trainer to come up and help him with Tooz.

Meanwhile, Pat goes outside to try to corral the big Amazon because he's terrorizing the hallway and he finally persuades him to come on back to the room for another drink. And just then there's a knock on the door and, thank God, it's the trainer.

Only problem was he's drunker than Matuszak. He falls face first into the room and in two minutes he's a stone.

Finally the doctor comes up and gives Tooz a shot of something to knock him out. They throw the trainer in the bed with Matuszak and they were as happy as a couple of clams the rest of the night.

After that they gave Toomay a single room.

PART THREE

☆ WINNING THE BIG ONE

CHAPTER TWELVE

FASTER THAN A SPEEDING LINEMAN

Dallas had a lot of great players. They have what they call the Ring of Honor where all the Cowboy greats are enshrined. And somebody asked me once, "When are they gonna put you in the Ring?"

Who are they kidding? They put one guy a year in there. Lilly was the first. Then Meredith and Howley and Staubach. They could pick fifteen a year and I'd never make it. They still got Cornell Green and Rayfield Wright and Blaine Nye to pick from. Hell, Lee Roy Jordan ain't made it yet, for Christ's sake. Then there's Jethro Pugh, D. D. Lewis, Cliff Harris, Charlie Waters. You can name guys all day long.

Ring of Honor? Hell, I'm just glad I got to play.

I've read several times that I was an All-Pro. Whenever my name is mentioned in an article or something they'll usually say, "Former All-Pro Walt Garrison said this or that."

Let me get the record straight. I was never All-Pro. I made the Pro Bowl a couple times. But, believe me, I was never All-Pro. If I was, you would have heard about it on the first page of this book.

But I got an excuse.

It was very tough to make All-Pro as a fullback because they don't differentiate between a halfback and a fullback when picking the All-Pro team. They just pick two running backs. And when you got guys like O. J. Simpson and Walter Payton who run for a couple thousand yards, you ain't gonna be making no All-Pro backfield with 800 or 900 yards. Even in my best years, they never said O.J. and Garrison in the same sentence. Hell, they never said it in the same paragraph. No, I take that back. I think I read one time where a sportswriter said, "Garrison sure ain't no O. J. Simpson."

The sportswriters pick the All-Pro teams and the Pro Bowl is picked by the players. So I've always felt it's a bigger honor to play in the Pro Bowl than to be All-Pro anyway. Of course, that's probably because I played in the Pro Bowl.

But there's just a lot more inconsistencies and inequalities in the All-Pro selection. When Simpson gains 2000 yards the sportswriters naturally make him an All-Pro. But if he comes back the next year and has a mediocre season, he's still on the team.

It's more of a popularity contest. But the players pick the Pro Bowl team. And if the players you play against think you're a good football player, in my mind that's one of the greatest compliments a football player can get.

But an even greater tribute than that is if your teammates think you're a good football player. If your teammates know you're doing everything you can to help the team win, that's the ultimate compliment. That's what I aimed for— the respect of my teammates.

Back when I was at Oklahoma State, if they'd told me I would be the starting fullback on the Dallas Cowboys, I would have said, "You're nuts!"

I didn't have any size, I didn't have any moves and I didn't have any speed. When they time you with a calendar, you're slow. But my college coach always used to tell me, "It ain't when you get there, it's *if* you get there. It don't matter if it takes you ten seconds to run ten yards as long as you get ten yards."

Actually, I wasn't the slowest guy on the Cowboys. Hey, I could daylight Blaine Nye. But I always lined up over by the linemen whenever we'd do sprints so I wouldn't look so slow. But even most of the linemen could outrun me. In fact, by my last season I was so slow there were only two guys on the whole team I could outrun—both linemen, of course. That's the starting running back for the Cowboys, a team that was known at the time as "Speed Inc."

One year at training camp they lined up all the veterans to run the 40. The first thing you do when you get there is run the Landry Mile to see if you're in shape. Then you run the 40's to see how fast you are. Now the rookies had already done all that because they'd been there for two weeks by the time the veterans showed up. So they were standing on the sidelines observing.

I was out there in my shorts and T-shirt and I'm feelin good. I'm in great shape and I'm ready to burn those 40's. This was my fifth or sixth year in the league. And Landry comes up to me and says, "That's all right, Walt, you don't have to run the 40's. We know what you can do."

"No, no, Coach, I'm ready."

"We don't want to tire you out, Walt."

"Coach, I'm feelin good. It's OK. I'm ready." I was pumped.

"Walt," he said, and he's sort of whispering to me with his arm on my shoulder, "look, if those rookies ever find out how slow you are and you've been playing for six years, they'll think it's a snap to make this team."

It's always nice when the coach has faith in your lack of ability.

Actually, I had only one real regret. I always said if I ever scored a TD standing up, I was gonna spike the ball. I had me a dance all worked out and everything. It never happened. I was never fast enough to get in there standing up. I always had two or three guys hanging all over me by the time I got there.

I broke loose one time in Philadelphia on a little swing pass and I had a wide-open field ahead of me. So I took off for paydirt and the whole time as I'm running down the field I'm thinking how I was gonna do a little two-step boogie in the end zone and spike the ball and then run over and give every fan in the front row a high-five hand slap. You know, the whole hotdog routine complete with mustard and relish.

And then a goddamn defensive tackle ran me down from behind. But the lucky SOB had the angle on me. He was directly behind me.

I think I ran 50 yards and he ran behind me stride for stride and finally caught my ass at the 5-yard line. That was depressing. Especially at the meeting the following Monday morning. When they showed the film all the linemen were cheering for the guy to catch me. And, of course, they played it about a dozen times and every time there'd be this big dumb sonuvabitch catching me from behind. Shit!

So how did a guy with no speed, no size, no talent—a fullback from a mediocre college team make it with the Dallas Cowboys? Luck. Lots and lots of luck.

When I came to Dallas they just happened to be looking for a fullback. Somebody who could help out if Perkins got hurt. Dallas was probably the only team in the NFL I could have played for. It was just the right team at the right time.

They needed a body to sit on the bench and watch Perkins run up and down the field and if by some chance he ever got hurt I'd be there. I wouldn't be a lot of use but I'd be there. I was an insurance policy.

But I was lucky. I sat around on the bench for a few years and that gave me the opportunity to develop as a football player.

A lot of great players don't make it in pro football because they go to the wrong team at the wrong time. If you get drafted by a team where they got two or three great running backs, it don't matter how good you are.

The funny thing is they cut guys all the time who I thought were better running backs than me. I'd think, "God dang, the guy can catch a football, he runs like hell, he's faster than me, bigger than me." And he'd be gone.

When they got players all over training camp every year who can do everything better than you, it don't take a genius to see the handwriting on the wall. Every year I thought, "God, they're gonna cut me." Even the year after we won the Super Bowl and I was selected to play in the Pro Bowl, I went to training camp thinking, "This is the year they're gonna cut me." I was scared to death.

Maybe it was good that I wasn't loaded with talent. I knew there was only one way I was going to survive. I had to do more and work harder than anyone else. I hustled every down. Every play I was like a madman.

Sometimes all that hustle can backfire on you though. One year in Philadelphia we lined up for a play where I ran a flare pattern out. The quarterback, Craig Morton, is supposed to fake a screen to the left and hit me with a flare pass to the right. Everybody is supposed to go to the screen but the linebacker covering me read that puppy all the way. He's standing there with me. Well, Morton sees him, so he decides to throw the football away. He flips it over my head out of bounds. At least he thought it was out of bounds. Until I jumped up and caught the damn thing with one hand. Made a hell of a catch. How was I supposed to know he was trying to throw it away? I figured he just threw a lousy pass.

So I made this great one-handed catch and just then the linebacker cremates me. Knocks me backward about 10 yards and spins me around in the air and somehow I come down on my feet. So I take off. I run 40 yards down the sidelines and, of course, some big lineman gets the angle on me again and pulls me down from behind about the ten.

And Morton runs up to me and he's pissed off. "What the hell do you think you're doing? I was throwing that ball away."

Here I thought I was a big hero and it turns out I've screwed up again.

I wasn't the only hard worker on the team, believe me. Some of the greatest players were also the hardest workers which isn't any big surprise. Talent and hard work make for greatness.

One very talented guy was Lance Alworth. He was one of the greatest wide receivers in the history of pro football. We got him from San Diego in 1971 and he helped us win a Super Bowl. Lance was slight and had a real light way of running on the balls of his feet like a deer so we called him "Bambi."

Alworth was very fast. He had great hands and great moves. Everything. Now you'd think a guy who was All-AFL, All-Pro, All-Everything, maybe he'd rest on his clippings a little. Maybe take it easy in practice. Not Alworth. That sonuvabitch worked every day in practice. And every day *after* practice. He'd corral anybody he could to stay after and throw him passes. He wouldn't just throw the ball back and forth. He'd run deep routes 40 or 50 yards downfield every time. Or he'd try to catch the ball looking right back over his shoulder or into the sun.

Bambi was an overachiever. He didn't think you were supposed to drop anything. If you touched it you were supposed to hang on to it. And mostly he did.

Lance helped me a lot with my pass catching. We used to throw the ball back and forth before practice and try to catch it with one hand or try to catch it in an odd position. We'd play catch on our knees or on our backs or standing on one leg.

Another hard worker was Raymond Berry, the legendary pass catcher for the Baltimore Colts, who's now the head coach of the New England Patriots. Landry hired Berry to be an assistant coach at Dallas when I was there. Talk about running routes! Catching a football was an exact science to Berry (and that ain't just throwing a term around). Johnny Unitas to Raymond Berry is probably the greatest pass-catching duo of all time. There was no guesswork between those two. Unitas knew exactly where Berry would be. When he ran a sideline pattern, it was so many steps, cut, so many more steps, and the ball was right there. He'd catch it, put his two feet down, step-step, and the next step he was out of bounds.

The first day Berry arrived at the Cowboy training camp he was demonstrating to the receivers how to run routes.

"OK, I'll show you all how to run a sideline pattern."

So Raymond lines up on the hash mark and runs down the field, dun, dun, dun, dun, dun, dun, breaks right, dun, dun, catches the ball . . . but he's out of bounds about a foot.

So he goes back, lines up, dun, dun, dun, dun, dun, dun, breaks, dun, dun, catches. And he's about a foot out of bounds.

He comes back and says to us, "The field is too narrow."

We all looked at him, "What?"

"The field is too narrow."

Ya, sure. We'd been at that facility in Thousand Oaks for five or six years at the time. Same practice field the whole time.

Berry goes over to Landry. "The field is too narrow, Tom."

"No, Raymond," Tom says. "We been out here forever."

But Berry just looks at Landry and says real matter of factly, "Either the hash marks aren't right or the field is too narrow." He wasn't mad or upset. He was just stating a fact.

So Tom shrugs and they go and get a tape measure and they measure the field and it's eleven inches too narrow.

We all looked at the tape and then we looked at each other and then we looked at Raymond Berry. And if we didn't know it before, we knew it then. We were looking at someone great.

Dave Manders was to centers what Berry was to pass catching. Manders was a free agent out of Michigan State who turned out to be the first Dallas center ever to go to the Pro Bowl. Dave worked hard every day and it paid off. He was a master at the center snap. He had total control of the ball.

The laces of the ball are supposed to be pointing away from the place kicker when he kicks the ball. On a long field goal whichever side the laces are on, the ball will tend to drift that way. So the holder gets the ball, places it down and spins the ball so the laces are pointing toward the end zone.

But Manders eliminated all that fiddling around. He knew exactly how many spins it took before the ball got to the holder. Dan Reeves was the holder at the time and Manders would snap the ball and the laces were right in the same exact spot every time. Not ninety out of one hundred. Every time. Reeves never had to spin the ball. He just caught it, the laces were right there and he put it down. That saved a couple tenths of a second, which often meant the difference between getting it off and getting it blocked.

Now that comes from hard work. Just doing it time after time after time after time. Until you get it right.

Another hard worker was Bob Hayes. Bob was the fastest man in the world but there was one little problem— when he joined the Cowboys he couldn't catch a football. So what good was he?

Well, Red Hickey, the Cowboys' receiver coach, worked with Bob and worked with him and Bob eventually developed a great pair of hands. If you look at the highlight films of the Cowboys when Bob was playing, you'll see him make some of the most unbelievable catches you ever saw. He was so fast that he just zips by the camera and the ball'd be in the air trying to catch up.

A lot of people ask me how fast Bob really was. Well, Bob won two Olympic gold medals and set the world record in the 100 at 9.1 seconds. I fell off a cliff one time that was 100 yards high and it took me longer than that to hit bottom.

One time Bob caught a pass against Spider Lockhart, the safety for the Giants. Now Spider was a speed burner. One of the fastest defensive backs ever to play. And Lockhart had the angle on Bob and Hayes just dusted off his ass for a TD. Spider never got any closer. In fact, he lost ground. Afterward they asked Hayes, "Weren't you worried that Lockhart was right behind you?"

And Bob said real casually, "No, he only runs a 9.3."

Lockhart was fast but he wasn't as fast as Bullet Bob. When you run a 9.1, a 9.3 looks like a sumo wrestler with bad knees.

The fastest man on earth. That was Bob Hayes. But, you know what, by the time he was through playing football, everybody thought of Hayes as a great All-Pro wide receiver who just happened to be pretty darn fast.

One of the reasons I lasted so long in pro football was because I wasn't injury prone. Take a guy like Claxton Welch who was a tough little halfback for the Cowboys. He was a much more talented runner than I was but he lasted two or three years and then, *adios.* Claxton was a little guy, all muscled up. He looked like a little Charles Atlas. He had muscles everywhere and he was fast. But all he had to do was bend over and he'd pop something. He pulled a muscle once tying his shoe. I never pulled a muscle in my life. You gotta have one to pull it.

When the Cowboys drafted Malcolm Walker out of Rice as a number-one draft choice, it scared me to death. Walker was big and fast. I remember the first time I saw Walker's legs. They were bigger than my whole body! He played a little while but his knee was screwed up. He'd get down in a stance and he'd have to stay there the whole game.

Garrison survives another one.

Another reason I stuck with the Cowboys was because I'd play hurt. Once I got into the starting lineup, I wouldn't let them take me out. It didn't matter how beat up I was. I knew if I went down with an injury, I might never get back in there.

See, if you ever get hurt, they got ten guys waitin who are as good or better than you are. But if you don't ever give them a chance to show the coaches what they can do, they'll never know how good these guys are.

D. D. Lewis was a great linebacker but he never got a chance to play for his first five years because they had three great linebackers ahead of him—Howley, Jordan and Edwards. And they never got injured. Well, what I mean is, they never got injured bad enough to keep them out on Sunday.

Edwards broke his wrist once and he played the next week. Howley played one year against the Colts with a separated shoulder. Baltimore had a screen pass that you could read from your easy chair. D.D. was ready to play. Howley was out of practice all week and D.D. was all ready to get himself an interception or two. Show Landry how good he was and push one of those guys outta there.

So game day comes and they strap Howley's shoulder down and he goes out and picks off two passes. And the whole game poor D.D.'s on the sidelines muttering, "Those were my goddamn interceptions. Those were my goddamn interceptions."

When D.D. finally did get to play, he turned out to be an All-Pro. But for a while all he was famous for was the dumbest statement ever made by a football player.

The first time we flew into St. Louis I was sitting next to D.D. He's looking out the window and he says, "You know, Walt, I didn't know St. Louis was the headquarters for McDonald's."

I couldn't figure out what the hell he meant. So I look out the window and there's the big arch, "The Gateway to the West."

"D.D.," I said, "you big dummy. There's only one arch there, pardner. McDonald's has two arches. That must be Burger King's headquarters. They're the guys with one arch."

"Oh, ya," he says, still looking out the window.

I had a reputation for being tough, for playing with a lot of injuries that would have kept a lot of other players on the bench. I probably wasn't that tough. I was just lucky enough that all my injuries looked bad but they weren't bad enough to force me out of the game. So after a while I got this bad-ass reputation. I'm sure that reputation helped me stay in the game longer. Some rookie would come in who was faster and bigger and better but Landry'd keep me because he knew I'd play no matter what. But like I say, it was a lot of luck. If they tear your kneecap off, you ain't playin, baby, no matter how tough you are because your leg ain't gonna do what you want it to do. But if you separate your shoulder or bang up a few ribs which I did a couple times then they can tape you up and you can play. It hurts like hell but you can play.

Now, I don't like pain. But they say some people have a low threshold and some have a high one. Evidently, mine is high. They used to ask me, "Doesn't it hurt?"

"Goddamn right it hurts."

Everything hurt. I'd have bruises all over me when a game was over. It looked like an army walked on me. Considering the beating I was supposed to have taken, I came out of football pretty good. But I don't think I probably got hit as hard as some other running backs. And that was my game—taking a hit. I used to think nobody could ever hurt me no matter how big they were.

Then I found out that was bullshit too. I got broken ankles, broken ribs, broken collarbones. But, luckily, I never had to miss a game because of those injuries. Actually, the worst injury I had was a pinched nerve. Every time I stood up I got dizzy. So I missed three or four games because I couldn't do anything without falling on my ass.

There is a difference between pain and injury and some players couldn't distinguish the difference. Football players play in pain. That's the business. If you play football, you gotta play in pain. That's why I don't think I'd enjoy playing today. It's changed so much. Guys are making so much money. They're not hungry. It hurts a little bit, they take the day off.

Now you take Walter Payton. That sonuvabitch played. People would say, "Payton never gets hurt." But he had to play hurt. You can't play running back and not play hurt. A running back gets hit on nearly every play. And Payton never ran out of bounds to avoid a hit. And he missed one game in twelve years! For my money, he's the greatest running back in history.

But football can be brutal, especially for the faint of heart. You hear stories about guys who got injured in football like Jim Otto who takes about an hour and a half to get out of bed in the morning because his knees are so shot. Or E. J. Holub who had sixteen knee operations. The doctor finally told him, "If you have another one, we'll just have to cut your leg off. You don't have nothing left."

They cut on my arm once and the team doctor, Dr. Knight, sewed me up with wire. A week or two later, I drove up to Dr. Knight's place with Bill Robinson to get the stitches taken out. Dr. Knight was doing a hip operation when I arrived and he comes into the room in a little green operating suit and he's bloody from his shoulders all the way down. Looks like he just butchered a hog.

"I ain't got but a second," he says. "Sit down on that table over there."

He went over to a table and looked through this old leather bag and came out with a goddamn old pair of wire pliers. He walked over and cut the end off that wire and got a hold of it and *wuuuuuuuuuuuuuppp*! Just jerked it out and said, "Get outta here. I don't wanna see you no more."

Bill was white as a sheet. "God dang," he says. "That's a doctor?"

Before a game one time I was laying on the trainer's table and Pat Toomay wandered in. Now Pat didn't have the highest confidence in our doctors anyway and when he comes in, I'm lying on the trainer's table with a needle about two feet long sticking in my sternum. They were gonna deaden some broken ribs with Novocaine. Well, one dose wasn't enough so the doctor unscrews the vial and there's this big ol needle sticking outta my chest while he goes and gets another vial. And Toomay is standing there sorta in shock with horror in his eyes and he says, "Holy crap! What am I doing here? That's going to be me in a few years."

Football is no place for a deep thinker.

CHAPTER THIRTEEN

JUST A PINCH

Don Perkins was my hero. He took Reeves and me under his wing and taught us a lot about running back. Ermal Allen was a good running-backs coach but a coach doesn't always have the time to get to all the little tiny details. And those are sometimes the things that make all the difference.

Perkins was unselfish enough so even if you were a rookie looking for his job, he'd teach you all he could. I asked Perk once, "Why are you trying to help me?"

"Walt," he said, "we've never done a thing in the play-offs. If you're a better player than I am, then you ought to be playing because I'll make more money that way. If you're not better than I am, then I should be playing."

When he retired, Perk was fifth on the NFL all-time rushing list so you know he could pack that pigskin. He wasn't fast but he was explosive. Nobody could beat him for 10 yards. Bob Hayes tried and Perk dusted him every time. Bob Hayes! Don Perkins was the world's fastest human for 10 yards. And when you're a running back, the first 10 yards is everything.

Another thing is Perk had crazy legs. When he ran they'd go every whichaway. So you couldn't grab on. I used to like to be behind him in the I formation and when they'd hand off to him, I'd just watch him go. He was funny to watch. Those legs'd go flying all over the place and then zap! he'd cut and he'd be through the hole.

Despite all those yards he gained, the thing Perk did best was block. He's the best blocking running back I've ever seen. There wasn't anybody even close. He had that unbeliev-able explosion. What they call the "short stroke." He'd just bend his knees a little and explode.

We used to have a pass-protection drill where the backs had to block our linebackers, and those veteran linebackers, Jordan and Howley and Edwards, would look over and see where Perkins was. "Let's see. One, two, three, four." They'd count off and make sure a rookie lined up with Perkins because they knew Perkins was gonna hurt you. They went after Garrison or Reeves—one of those wimps. No way they wanted to take on Perkins. He'd just crush you!

My first year with Dallas I knew I couldn't start. The second year I thought I could have played. Maybe not pushed Perkins completely outta there. But at least shared some playing time with him. Now my third year I definitely thought I was good enough to start over Perkins. Looking back, I know I wasn't.

My third year was frustrating because I really wanted to play. When we'd get a good lead in the game, I couldn't understand why Landry wouldn't put me in and rest Perkins. I wanted to show him what I could do. But he didn't give a damn what I could do.

Finally, in 1969, my fourth year with the Cowboys, I started. That was because Perkins finally retired. Thank God. If Perkins had played five more years, I would probably still be on the bench.

Landry believed that a player earned his starting position. In order to replace a starter, you not only had to be better than he was that week, you had to be better than he was two, three, four, five weeks. And he had to be performing like spit. A guy could run up and down the field one game, look like Jim Brown, O.J. and Payton all rolled into one dream running back and the next Monday at practice he'd still be on the second team running the dummy drills. That was Landry's way.

Now, me, I didn't earn my spot at all. Perk retired and I was the next one in line. I won it by default. In other words, my luck was still holding out.

But I didn't inherit just Perkins' starting-fullback position. I also got his endorsements. The first commercial I ever did was for a breakfast sausage. Perk was doing the radio spots for Carl's Tasty Sausage and when he retired, they called me to take his place. Hey, I was the Dallas fullback. The fullback for the Cowboys did the Carl's Tasty Sausage commercials. It was some kind of unwritten rule.

First, I did a few radio spots and then they decided to do a TV commercial. And that was the first time the world got to see the face that was voted Most Handsome at Lewisville High.

So even my rise to TV stardom was another lucky deal.

Over the years I did commercials for Tony Lama Boots, Dodge Trucks, Burris Mills Light Crust Flour. And then snuff came along. And with it the slogan that made me famous, "Just a pinch is all it takes."

Some guy from NFL films called me. They were doing a film on three professional football players who had unusual off-season pursuits. Carl Eller of the Vikings was an actor. Ben Davidson of the Oakland Raiders rode motorcycles. They asked me to be the third guy because I rodeoed.

They put together a film called *The Hunters.* The premise being that the three of us were still hunting something in the off-season. Why do you hunt? Why do you do the crazy things you do?

They came to Mineral Wells, Texas, to a professional rodeo I was entered in. They showed up two or three days before the rodeo started and they took pictures of me driving up in my truck, unlocking my gear, bullshittin with the other cowboys and bulldoggin.

Well, on the dashboard of my truck there were about twenty cans of Skoal and a spittoon that my mother gave me when I was still in college. I still got the damn thing up on my dashboard. So they had me dip some snuff which I'd been doing before I even knew who made it. There was probably thirty, forty seconds in the film of me talking about dippin snuff.

Anyway, the film came out on national TV and, at that time, the folks at U.S. Tobacco had never done a TV commercial. They'd advertised in the trade papers but never on TV. Well, as my luck would have it, they were looking for someone to do a commercial. One of the guys at the ad agency in New York handling the Skoal account saw *The Hunters* and told them Walt Garrison is the guy you need. He's a real cowboy and he plays football for the Cowboys and he's been dippin snuff since he was a puppy.

So the bigshots at U.S. Tobacco called me to see if I'd do a commercial for them. I went to talk to Al Ward of the Cowboys and I asked him, "Is there any problem with me doing a snuff commercial?"

I knew as an active football player you could not do ads for cigarettes or hard liquor or beer. You used to be able to but you can't now. That's why they've got retired athletes on those Miller Lite commercials. But like I say you used to. I still got a program from a rodeo in 1941 and there's Joe

DiMaggio puffin on a Lucky Strike. Looks weird but back then they were all doing it.

But U.S. Tobacco handles only smokeless tobacco—Skoal and Copenhagen snuff. So I asked Al if there was any problem representing those products.

"No," he said, "but we don't think you should do it because it would be bad for your image."

So I called U.S. Tobacco back and told em I couldn't do it. At the time my life was football. I thought I was gonna be playing until I was at least fifty. Maybe fifty-five.

I told them it was all right to do the commercial but at this time the Cowboys didn't think it was right for my career or image or some damn thing. And Dallas was paying my checks then.

They said, "Fine."

And I figured that was it. But my luck was still holdin. Because instead of getting somebody else to do their commercials, they waited a year and called me back.

This time they offered me ten grand. Holy shit! That was a lot of dough. I was only making about thirty. And this was gonna be for one commercial.

So I called Al Ward back. "There ain't nothin in there that says I can't do it, is there?"

"No."

"Well, you're worried about it hurting my image. God-damn, y'all been billing me as the 'Cowboys' Cowboy.' Rodeo and whittlin and dippin snuff. That *is* my image. So I'm gonna do it."

And I did and the relationship just kept building from there. I not only became the TV and radio spokesman for U.S. Tobacco but eventually, after I retired, I went to work full-time for them.

It wasn't all smooth sailing with Skoal. I did my best to screw up and managed to do it more than once.

Before I ever went to work for U.S. Tobacco, before I ever did the first commercial, they had me as a guest at the National Association of Tobacco Distributors convention in Miami. Everybody from all over the industry shows up. They paid me to come out there and sign autographs and shake hands and stuff. They also had a luncheon every day and each luncheon was sponsored by a different company. And this particular day it was U.S. Tobacco's turn. They had me and Nick Buoniconti from the Miami Dolphins get up and welcome everyone to the lunch. There were about twelve hundred of them there. Well, you know how convention food is. They prepare it a week ahead, then they freeze it and, of course, it ain't worth a damn.

So Nick got up and he's real eloquent. He welcomed them all there and thanked them for coming. Then he introduced me. I got up, said it was nice to be there, blah, blah, blah. . . . Then I said, "You know, this food reminds me a lot of the food Mama used to make when I was living at home. Only she didn't shit in it afterward."

And there is dead silence. The tobacco industry is an old family owned and operated establishment of companies. And nobody had ever said "shit" at a tobacco convention before. Ever.

There wasn't a peep in the place for about thirty seconds but it seemed like an hour and a half. I was standing there thinking "Holy cow. I've screwed up. I'll never work for this company. And there goes the commercial deal too."

U.S. Tobacco had a table right down in front and I looked down and there was L. A. Bantle, the chairman of the board and all the officers of the company. And Mr. Bantle is on his knees laughing. Well, if you know anything about corporations, when the chairman laughs, all the vice presidents laugh right along with him. Pretty soon the whole place broke up.

That's a story you still hear at all the tobacco conventions because everybody was thinking it but nobody was stupid enough to say it. Except me, of course. I was a big hit from then on. But then again, I haven't been asked to speak anymore and that was fifteen years ago.

Years later I blew it even worse. I was driving back to my hotel room from a bar in Oklahoma City. I was up there representing the company in an important court case. We'd been in that courtroom from nine o'clock in the morning till five every day. You can't even piss unless the judge lets you. You have a break at noon and a break in the afternoon. That's it.

I'd been up there like four or five weeks by then every day, five days a week. And it was driving me up a tree. So one evening we all go up to this little beer joint/restaurant in Edmond to eat and have a drink. So I started drinking a little Scotch. And it turned into a lot of Scotch.

Along about one o'clock I decided to go on back to the hotel room. So I get in the car and I'm driving along on this big ol wide four-lane street and I'm takin it easy, going maybe 45 or 50 mph. Just driving along and the red lights come on behind me. The cops. I thought, "What the hell. I'm not speeding or nothin."

So I pull over and get out and the cop says, "This is a thirty-five miles per hour speed zone. You been drinkin?"

"Yes, sir."

"OK," he says, "here's what I want you to do. Hold your arms out to your side and stand on one leg and pick the other one up like that." He looked like a goddamn flamingo with one finger up his nose and the other up his rear.

And I looked at him and said, "Ain't a sonuvabitch alive can do that."

They took me downtown and I paid $108 bail and then I called our lawyers. "Oh, goddamn, Walt," they yelled, "not in the middle of this court case. Get outta there as quick as you can. We'll do what we can."

So they sent over a lawyer from Edmond and I was sitting out on the curb in front of the station like a bad boy. And he went inside and talked to the police to try to keep it quiet. But, of course, they found out about it anyway and it was splashed all over the papers: "WALT GARRISON, FOR-MER COWBOY, FOUND DRUNK."

Oh, shit.

Luckily for me, there was this smart ol lawyer headin up our case named Austin Jennings. All the other lawyers were going nuts. "How could you do something like this, Walt?"

"Whadda ya mean?" I said. "I been up here for five goddamn weeks! Whadda you talkin about, how could I do this? Shit, I stayed sober for a month."

And Austin says, "Wait a minute. That was probably one of the smartest things any of us have done."

The other lawyers looked at Austin. "What?"

"It'll just show the jury that you're human, Walt. Don't even worry about it."

From then on the rest of them never said a word about it. And a bit later when Austin won the case for us, they were coming up to me, "Hey, way to go, Walt. Way to get drunk."

I think Joe Namath permanently damaged the credibility of athletes in commercials when he did that pantyhose commercial. Now everybody knows Joe Namath don't wear pantyhose except in that commercial. And they know he only did it for one reason—money.

In fact, shortly after that the Screen Actors Guild and the American Federation of Television and Radio Artists passed a bylaw that said when you do a commercial now you have to sign a piece of paper that says you actually use that product. You don't have to use it regular but you have to have at least used it.

It's all a matter of credibility. One thing that doesn't have credibility is Joe Namath in drag.

That's the reason I've never done a commercial for a product I don't use. It's easy for me to do a snuff commercial because I've used Skoal for years.

One time a guy called me from Natural Light beer to do a commercial for them. They offered me $25,000 to do the commercial—a thirty-second spot—and I told them, "I don't drink that beer."

"Why not?"

"Cause I don't like it."

"Well, we're gonna send you some and see if it'll grow on you."

They sent twenty cases over and I like to never get rid of it.

So then they called back a few months later and this time they offered me $40,000.

"I appreciate it a lot," I told them. "But I can't do it."

A lot of people said, "Why, you must be nuts. I'd drink turpentine for forty grand."

"That might be," I said. "Some people'd skin their mother for a sawbuck. But that ain't me."

I don't know what I'd be doing today if I hadn't hooked up with U.S. Tobacco. Most players don't plan for what they're gonna do after they get done playing football. I was one of them. I never thought about life after football for the first four or five years I was playing. I didn't even try to do anything. I thought, "Heck, I'm gonna play forever."

But reality dawns on you the first time you get hurt. You recover from your injury and you're there at the game ready to play and the team goes on without you. Maybe even better without you. You realize real sudden like that you're not indispensable.

When Lilly retired I thought, "Gal dang, how they gonna replace Lilly?" And along came Randy White. When Mel Renfro retired, Charlie Waters was right there to take his place and Everson Walls took Charlie's place.

A big problem for a pro athlete is he never knows when his career is gonna end. If you signed up for eight or ten years and that's how long you were gonna be a football player, you could plan ahead for the day you retired. But you don't know if you're gonna last fifteen years or fifteen minutes. You can be going along having the greatest year of your life, making big dough, running for 1500 yards and somebody hits you and you land on your knee wrong—and your career is over. You've played your last football game except on Christmas with your kids out in the street.

They might have had you penciled in at halfback for the next five years and Monday morning you ain't got a job. So preparing for the future in the real working world is tough for a pro football player. You can't go to a company and say, "Hey, hold this here job for me for ten years, will you?"

It always appears to the public that there are a lot of opportunities for endorsements for a pro athlete. And there are if you're one of the top stars. But for most athletes there just aren't that many jobs or endorsements staring him in the face. Hey, if you're O.J. or Joe Willie, yeah, the world is your oyster but if you're Dave Edwards or Dave Manders, both great players, you don't get diddly.

A lot of players tried to start businesses when they were still playing. But that's no cinch deal either.

When Mike Ditka, the coach of the Chicago Bears, played for Dallas in the early seventies, he opened a dinner-dance club in Dallas called The Sportspage, and I mean it did unbelievable business. People were lined up on the sidewalk every night begging to get a table. And on Sundays after the game, you couldn't buy your way in. See, that's where all the players went after the game and, of course, that attracted a crowd real quick. They'd get to drink and dance *and* see all their football heroes close up. That went on for two and a half years.

All of a sudden Ditka thought he was a restaurant tycoon, instead of just a damn good tight end. So Ditka took his profits and went out and opened up a joint in Richardson, Texas, called The Hungry Hunter. They served wild boar, bear meat, quail—stuff like that. Hell, they even had ostrich eggs, for Christ's sake.

Oh, man, when they opened that place Mike figured he'd retire in two years. But the damn place didn't do nothing. I mean how many times do you say to your wife, "Geez, honey, you know what I really feel like tonight? An ostrich egg!"

After that fiasco Ditka bought some land in Wolf Creek Pass and opened up a ski area. I don't know what Mike thought he knew about skiing but, I'll tell you, it wasn't enough. They didn't get any snow the first year and *adios* investment. The place bombed.

So, in the end, he blew most of the money he'd made at The Sportspage trying to hit another big one. Before he knew it, there he was back at tight end with nothing in the bank and a few good years left in him. Good thing he knew how to coach.

But, believe me, Ditka wasn't the only one who blew a bundle on some half-baked business deal. John Niland got roasted in the barbecue business. Ralph Neely opened a nightclub called The Pearl Street Warehouse and, naturally, it did rotten business. Dave Edwards put a bunch of money into a cosmetics company for his wife called The House of Turtle. Went into the soup in months. Then he sank all his money into a giant-chocolate-chip-cookie company. Damn thing crumbled in front of his eyes.

Then there are the guys like Charlie Waters who finally decided to play it smart, forget the get-rich-quick schemes, play it close to the vest—and it still backfired on them.

D.D. and Charlie did a Miller Lite beer commercial when they first retired. They paid them a bundle to do the spot. Then they said they'd pay them $2000 every time they made a personal appearance for Miller.

Ben Davidson toured with the Miller Lite All-Stars. Made about a hundred appearances a year, signing a few autographs, playing some celebrity softball games. That kind of stuff. And for his trouble he made well over a quarter million a year. Plus expenses.

At the time, Charlie had an offer from Roger Staubach to go to work for Roger's real estate firm. So he said, "Ah, hell, I'm not gonna do it. I'm gonna turn the corner. I'm going to get into business." That was Charlie's favorite expression back then. "I'm gonna turn the corner."

Damned if I know which corner he was talking about. But it wasn't Easy Street, I can tell you that. A couple years went by and Charlie got to hurting for money and he asked D.D., "Think they'd want us to do some more commercials for them?"

"Hell, ya, let me call."

Well, D.D. calls the Miller Lite people and they're all excited because they'd been looking for somebody with a little youthful sex appeal. And Charlie's a good-looking kid. They want to shoot a commercial that week and do some radio spots. The deal was worth about $80,000. For starters.

So Charlie asked his boss Staubach if it'd be all right with him and Roger, who can really have a pretty straight stick up his ass at times, told Charlie, "No, if you do that you can't work here anymore."

So Charlie turned it down.

Now I tell you, I think I woulda had to take that deal.

After D.D. and Charlie made their first commercial, Lorimar Films out in Hollywood saw it and they loved them in it. So they asked Charlie and D.D. to go out and do a screen test for a pilot series. It was gonna be *The Texas Rangers.* They were supposed to be cops on motorcycles out in Texas.

Somebody asked D.D., "I didn't know you football players could act?"

"Oh, hell yes," he said. "I acted like a football player the last four years I played."

Anyway, Lorimar sent them a script and Charlie read it. D.D. was to Charlie what George Andrie was to Lilly.

"Whadda you think, Charlie?"

"Ah, hell, I'm gonna turn the corner. To hell with this shit. I'm gonna turn the corner."

"Well, whatever you say, Charlie. I guess I'll turn it down too."

They might have turned down as much as a couple million dollars in that deal. Whew! For real estate?

CHAPTER FOURTEEN

THE COWBOYS' COWBOY

During the first five years I played football for Dallas, the only job I had in the off-season was rodeoin.

My event was steer wrestlin, also known as bulldoggin. They say a black cowboy named Bill Pickins originated bulldoggin. When he brought a steer down he was supposed to have bit him in the lip with his teeth and he threw him thataway. In fact, they had a standing bet he could throw and hold down any steer for five minutes with his teeth—and he never lost. That's probably a lie but I've heard it at least a thousand times around rodeos.

The object of steer wrestlin is to twist a steer down by the horns and neck to the ground until he's lying flat on his side with his head and all four feet pointing in the same direction. The fastest time wins.

It takes a lot of athletic ability to steer wrestle. Those steers weigh anything from 500 to 700 pounds. And there's no way anyone is strong enough to actually throw one down physically. It's like a throw in judo. You bring a steer's head around and you get his body weight working against him and then you turn his head back the other way. It's kind of like crackin a whip. If you do it right, he just falls.

Of course there are a lot of bad things that can happen too. If you throw one down wrong, you can get walked on real quick. Seven hundred pounds of walked on.

Actually, when I first started going to rodeos way back in junior high school, my events were bronc riding and bull riding. But when I was a professional cowboy, I was strictly a steer wrestler because I got too big to ride bareback horses and bulls. Most bull riders and saddle bronc riders weigh maybe 145 to 150. If they're real big, they'll weigh 170. At close to 200, I was way too big.

And way too smart.

Bull riding is a young man's sport. When you're thirty, you're an old bull rider. You might still be able to do it but by the time you get to be thirty, you're too smart to want to get up on one of those bulls.

The last time I rode a bull I was a senior in college. When I started playing with the Cowboys, they asked me to stop riding bulls which was all right with me. I was looking for an excuse to stop and still save face. "Oh, heck, I can't do this any more. Damn it. The Cowboys won't let me."

Thank God for the Cowboys.

The first time I wrestled a steer was at a junior rodeo in Livingston, Texas. It was one of those deals where the entry fee was six or seven bucks and you could enter as many events as you wanted for the same price.

My best friend, Bill Robinson, was in the ropin and bulldoggin and I was in the bronc riding and bull riding. So he said, "Why don't you get in the bulldoggin? It won't cost you nothin."

"I don't know how."

"What difference does it make? It don't cost you any more. You might get lucky and throw one down."

Well, I didn't get lucky that night but I found I really liked it and after that I started practicing for it. Before long, that became my event.

Me and Bill were like brothers. He'd stay at my house and I'd stay at his. He had a truck and a horse trailer and I didn't, so we used to go to the rodeo in his rig. And a lot of times we'd end up sleeping in that horse trailer because we couldn't afford a motel room. We'd feed the horses, tie them up to the trailer and go to the dance at the VFW. Then we'd come on home and get in the back, but first we'd drink enough beer so wherever we slept it was comfortable.

Bill was with me all the way. When I was doing commercials Bill was in every one. When I made the deal with Dodge trucks, they said we're gonna pay you so much money and I said, "OK, but I want a couple things. First, I wanna fly first class and I wanna car."

"No problem."

"And I wanna bring Bill Robinson along."

"What for?"

"Because the guy's been with me right along."

"We can't do that."

"Well, then forget it."

The money they were gonna pay me a year was nice but if Bill can't come, keep it. That was my attitude.

They called me back the next week and said, "You got it."

Bill wound up being in every commercial. He'd be standing around and they'd say, "You got anybody that can ride a horse in the background?"

"What's it pay?" Bill'd ask.

"Three hundred an hour."

"Ya, I believe I can handle that."

Everybody loved Bill. He was just a good guy. You could sit and talk with the sonuvabitch and you wouldn't be talking about nothing but you'd learn something. He was like a country philosopher.

Bill always used to talk to me about marrying a rich girl. "You know," he said, "if there's a spark of love in you, that money'll bring it out."

Me and Bill had a lot of good times together. We drank a lot of beer, wrestled a lot of steers, chased a lot of girls. But the thing we probably did the most was laugh.

My son Marty got a reputation among the kids at school that he liked to lie a little cause he was always telling everybody that Roger Staubach came over for dinner last night. That sorta stuff. And nobody believed him. Hell, Marty was on a first-name basis with Roger and these kids worshipped Staubach like he was a god.

Anyway, one day Marty's school had a Pet Day. Every kid was supposed to bring a pet to show off. Well, at the time, I had a llama and Marty said, "I'm bringing my llama."

Tony was this llama's name. You know, Tony Llama.

Well, all the kids said, "Ya, sure, your llama. And I suppose Roger Staubach is gonna ride it over here."

So Bill and I hauled that sucker over there the next day. That cleared up just about everything. If you can show up with a llama, what the hell, I guess it ain't no big deal to have Roger Staubach over for dinner.

Now how I got the llama's another story. Bill and I were in Martin, Tennessee, at this guy's house drinking his beer and he said, "Y'all don't need a llama, do you?"

I said, "You goddamn right I need a llama. I ain't got one. You got one?"

"Ya."

"Ah, bullshit."

"I do. Right out there in the barn."

So we go out there and, sure enough, he's got a llama that he bought somewhere.

"Whadda ya want for it?"

"Five hundred."

"I ain't got no way to get him home."

Well, this guy had this trailer sitting in the yard and Bill says, "Whadda ya gonna do with that trailer?"

"Oh, I been trying to sell it."

"I'll tell you what. I'll take the trailer. Walt'll take the llama. You put the llama in the trailer and deliver it to Lewisville, Texas, we'll buy it."

"Well," he says, "I got to come by there in about two weeks. I'll damn sure do it."

"We'll pay you when you git there," Bill says.

"Fair enough."

So me and Bill leave and the next morning at breakfast when I'm sober I say, "Bill, that guy ain't gonna actually bring that llama and that trailer down to Lewisville, is he?"

"Why, hell no! He's the biggest bullshitter in Tennessee and Tennessee's full of bullshitters."

Well, sure enough two weeks later the guy calls from Kansas City. He's up there looking for an elephant to buy.

"I'll be there in three days," he says. And the following Friday he pulled up in front of my office, unloaded the trailer and the llama and drove off to Florida to pick up a tiger.

So that's how my son got to be a hit at Pet Day.

Bill and I were something with the ladies too. One time we had us two hairdressers. These were good-lookin girls. Had those big ol beehive hairdos and made up like a couple Japanese actors. *Oooooo-weeeeee!* We had us something.

Well, earlier that day we had gone over to this practice bulldoggin pit and we was rasslin steers. We didn't have no extra clothes or nothing so when these two beauties picked us up, we had shit all over us. When we got in their car they kinda moved over to one side.

They took us to a favorite beer joint of mine called The Cow Palace. After we were there a bit, me and Bill get up to dance with them but they tell us, "Wait just a minute. We're going to the bathroom. We'll be back in no time." And they take off.

Me and Bill look at each other with big grins, "Man, this is gonna be a gooood deal. They love us."

To this day, right up to this very minute, I ain't never seen those two gals since.

Bill died February 27, 1985 at age thirty-nine. A blood vessel burst in his brain and that was it.

He died in a rodeo ring sitting there sippin on a beer, waiting for his turn at a steer. They said he just keeled over and died right there. I tell you he was never happier than when he was at a rodeo, so he musta died happy.

U.S. Tobacco set up an educational scholarship in Bill's name and we give it away at the College National Finals to the steer wrestler who earns the most money at the finals.

I miss Bill. He was a good one.

Rodeo is the original American sport. It predates baseball, football, basketball. All of them. And it's probably the only truly American sport. It came from a cowboy's ranch life, the work he did on the ranch. Ropin calves and steers. He had to brand em and doctor em out on the range which meant he had to ride and rope good and be able to tie a calf down. Bronc riding is another rodeo event that originated when they had to break the colts.

They say the first rodeo was held in Pecos, Texas. Naturally, everybody wanted to prove they were the best cowboy around. So three big ranches got together to see who had the best cowboys. Rodeo evolved from that.

Bull riding, bareback riding and other rodeo events that didn't have nothing to do with ranch work came later. Steer wrestlin, for instance, is strictly a macho, see-who-can-do-it kind of event. Nobody's gonna jump on the back of a steer and try to take him down on a ranch. Less he's got a lot of spare energy he's just dying to use up.

Twenty years ago the only cowboys you saw in the PRCA (Professional Rodeo Cowboy Association) were cowboys who were raised on a ranch, who had been around that life. Working cowboys out on the range.

Then you started seeing rodeo schools. And now you've got cowboys like Bobby Del Vecchio who finished second for the world championship in bull ridin two or three times. He's from the Bronx, New York. Gary Leffew was a hippie from California and somebody dared him to ride a bull and he got up there and he ain't hardly been down since. Turned out to be world champ.

Probably the biggest name that grew up in town is a guy named Charley Sampson. First of all, he's black. Secondly, he's from the Watts section of L.A. So there's a lot of rodeo cowboys who never were anywhere near a ranch growing up and they liked rodeo and ended up as professional cowboys.

Rodeo cowboys come from all kinds of places and backgrounds but the one thing they all have in common, I think, is their love of freedom. What I liked about rodeo was being able to do what I wanted to do, go where I wanted to go.

It's a great life.

The main problem with rodeo is it's so tough to survive financially out on the road. Like Bill used to say, "Rodeo is a great way of life. Too bad you can't make a living at it."

There just ain't that much money in rodeo. A few years back Monty Henson, who at that time was the world champion saddle bronc rider, said it cost him $24,000 to break even on the road. And the dollar went a lot farther then. He made thirty grand that year so he actually made $6000.

That's a good way to get a divorce. You're gone all the time and you can't make any money.

Now you know why they say, "Don't let your daughter marry a cowboy."

If I could have made the money in rodeo that I made in pro football I probably would have bulldogged for years. Too bad. I love rodeo. I won some money rodeoin. Not a lot. But I always had a hell of a good time.

I got a lot of publicity being a rodeo cowboy and playing for the Cowboys. Now if I'd played for the Dolphins or something, I'm sure no one would have cared if I rodeoed. But being a Cowboy and a *cowboy* was a public relations man's dream. Plus, in Texas there's more rodeoin than in any other state, so rodeo was popular with the Cowboy fans. And vice versa.

Cody Bill Smith was national saddle bronc champion three times and he was the biggest Dallas Cowboy fan in the world. He was a guide up in the wilderness outside Cody, Wyoming. Lived back up there in the woods in a cabin. Didn't even have a TV set. But when the Cowboys played, he'd get on a horse and ride twenty or thirty miles in the snow to town and rent him a motel room just so he could watch the game on TV. Then after the game he'd get back on his horse and ride back up to his cabin.

I remember the year I retired I was at the National Rodeo Finals and Cody come up to me in a bar. "Walt," he said, "gal dang, I'm sorry you quit. I'll tell you, they just ain't gonna be able to replace you."

"Well, thank ya, Cody."

"Ya, it'd be real hard to find someone dumb enough to just keep stickin' their head in there time after time and gettin hisself killed."

The damn thing about it, Cody meant it as a compliment.

The Cowboys never hassled me much about rodeoin. Coach Landry came to the rodeo one night to see how dangerous it was. I was in the calf ropin and steer wrestlin. And nothing bad happened. Ninety-nine times out of a hundred it doesn't. So they let me rodeo.

But Landry told me, "You know there's a clause in your contract that if you get hurt rodeoing we don't have to pay you." Which there was. It's a standard clause about participating in other sports.

I told him, "Ignorance is what makes any sport dangerous." The more you know about any sport, the less dangerous it is. Guys who race motorcycles think it's the safest thing in the world. Fighter pilots think nothing of going Mach-2 upside down. Now to me that ain't safe. Those sonuvabitches is crazy. At least I think so. But they don't. They think riding a 2000-pound bull is about the looniest thing you could ever do. And maybe it is.

So Landry let me rodeo. As long as I kept it to the off-season.

I tried to show a few Cowboys how to be cowboys. They were always after me to teach them to bulldog or rope or something.

One time Lee Roy and Meredith and Morton all wanted to try bulldoggin. So they come up to my father-in-law's ranch. I got one of the bulls out and got him by the tail so he couldn't run and they each tried to throw him down. They never got on a horse or anything like that. I had him by the tail and they'd sneak up on him, grab him by the horns and try to bring him down. Lee Roy did all right but the bull threw Meredith and Morton around like a couple of rag dolls.

Another time Dave Edwards came up and he said, "Boy, I wanna get a bunch of pictures of me riding a horse and catchin one of them steers."

So I said, "Fine."

So he gets up on the horse and he's ready to go and we let the steer go and it just about scared him to death. He didn't know the horse was gonna take off full-bore when the steer was turned loose.

He trots back up to us and he's kinda pale. "Holy shit! Hold it right there. This ain't exactly the way I thought it was gonna be now. I can't do this."

But Dave still wanted his pictures. So he had me take a picture of him in the chute ready to take off. Then a picture of him when he broke out. Then he had me and Bill catch a steer and throw him down and in the next picture Dave was on the ground holding the steer like he throwed it.

Another time Meredith called me and wanted to know if I could teach him how to ride.

"Ya, sure," I said. "How long you got?"

"Oh, just today."

"No way."

"Walt, look," he says, "I got this part in a movie. And all I got to do is ride a horse into town and get off in front of this saloon and go in there and do my little scene. Then, I get back on a horse and ride back out of town. The only thing is, I don't want to bounce."

This was after Don had retired and he was doing *Monday Night Football* and he started to do some movies. I believe this one was called *Banjo Hackett.* I'm not sure though because Meredith made so many of those lousy films back then I mix them up.

"Oh, hell, come on up," I said.

So he came up and he rode all day, nine or ten hours. We rode, ate lunch and rode some more. Finally he said, "I gotta go."

He could hardly walk. He had on some old double-knit pants and his little legs were raw and kinda bleeding when he left.

Well, anyway, toward the end of the day, Bill Weston, the foreman of the place, come by where we were riding. And Meredith come over to Bill and he said, "Bill, whadda ya think?"

And Weston, who is from West Texas, just an ol cowboy, said, "Well, I'll tell ya, Don. Ya probably oughta get Walt to double for ya. Or do a war movie."

People used to ask me all the time when I was playing which is tougher, football or rodeo? Well, football is tougher simply because it lasts longer.

A play in football lasts between four to six seconds. A typical bulldoggin run lasts about the same length of time. For that period of time the football player and the rodeo cowboy exert about the same amount of energy, the same effort. You've got to be a great athlete to excel at either sport at the top level.

The real difference is that the amount of time a football player actually performs in a game is so much longer than a cowboy at a rodeo. If you went to the finals at a rodeo, the most animals you'd ever run would be three. So the most you'd ever be out there in the arena would be fifteen to twenty seconds total.

Now if you're a starter in a football game, you'll be playing thirty minutes of hard football. That's what makes football a hell of a lot tougher than rodeo. You've got to be in so much better shape to play football.

When I got done playing a football game, I hurt everywhere. I could barely move. They'd lower me into a whirlpool and I'd drink about six beers just to ease the pain. When I got done rodeoin I was ready to go to the VFW Hall and dance all night.

The only thing I wanted to do all night after a football game was sleep.

One thing that's tougher about rodeo is the bars the cowboys hang out in. I used to go to The Rustler's Rest over in Fort Worth when I was playing for the Cowboys. It's the kind of bar where they check you for a gun when you go in and if you ain't got one, they give you one. A hold em and hit em place.

If you lock up with one of the barmaids you're safe because they can whip anyone that walks through the door, including you. The first prerequisite for becoming a barmaid at Rustler's is to be able to bench press more than Randy White. They ain't that good-lookin right off. But along about one or two o'clock they start to look like Miss Texas.

Wednesday night was "Prayer Meeting" at Rustler's. It was $4 a head, all the beer you can drink and bring your knife.

Jerry Lane used to play over there five, six nights a week with his band. And when a fight would break out they kept right on playing. They'd just play a little louder is all. And there was usually three, four fights a night. Good ones too!

I took Charlie Waters over to Rustler's one night to see a guy named Bear Creek. Bear Creek was about 4'11" with a big ol beard that hung down to his chest and a pot belly you could stack a case of beer on. He had a septic-tank business and on the side of his truck he had a sign painted, "Your shit is my bread and butter."

Bear Creek's claim to fame was that he could lay on his back and spit on the ceiling. Now Rustler's looked like an old converted barn with wooden floors and a ceiling that musta been eleven or twelve feet up. It was a hell of a feat. I mean he didn't just barely make it either. He spit on that ceiling laying down like you and I spit on the sidewalk. It splattered when it hit. There was brown spots all over the ceiling at

Rustler's because Bear Creek would chew and spit. People used to come from miles to see Bear Creek perform. Damn guy was a celebrity.

The night Charlie was there a guy came out and announced, "All right, Bear Creek's gonna spit on the ceiling now."

Everybody crowded around to watch him and he stood up and *patuwee!* he spat on the ceiling. No big deal. Nobody cheered, just a little polite applause.

So then he laid on his back and the crowd kinda backed up into a bigger circle to give him some spittin room. So Bear Creek goes *patuweee!* And the next thing you know there's flashlights trained on the ceiling and they're yelling, "There it is! There it is!" Like they'd discovered an oil well or something. And there's this old glob of spit hanging from the ceiling and everybody cheered their heads off like this sonuvabitch just cleared twenty feet in the pole vault.

Charlie couldn't believe it. "They didn't cheer that loud when I ran that interception in for a TD in the Redskins game."

CHAPTER FIFTEEN

JOLLY ROGER

From 1966 to 1969, the Cowboys went 42-12-1 and won their division all four years. But we somehow got hung with a loser's tag. We lost the NFL championship to Green Bay in 1966 and 1967 in the last seconds of two historic nail-biters. Then in 1968 and 1969 we lost the Eastern Conference playoff game to Cleveland, a team we were supposed to beat easily both times.

Everyone started saying we couldn't win the important games. "Dallas can't win 'the Big One.' " That was the rap on us.

I thought it was a truckload of fertilizer. A lot of teams would love a chance just to play in a Big One. Besides, we were in the playoffs eight straight years. So we musta won a few big ones along the way.

It's something a sportswriter dreamed up when he needed to fill a column, and everybody picked up on it. The implication was that we somehow psyched out in the pressure of important games. Psychology has won very few football games. Football is still blocking and tackling. If it was a game of psychology, psychologists would play the game. Instead of Dick Butkus, you'd have Joyce Brothers at middle linebacker.

I just never bought all that crap they wrote. What if we'd won those two games against Green Bay? Would they have said Lombardi's Packers can't win the Big One? What nonsense. The Green Bay legend and Dallas's bad rap all started with those great games.

In 1966 we played the Packers in Dallas and we were down 14–0 before our offense ever touched the ball. They took the opening kickoff and drove 80 yards and scored. Then they kicked off, we fumbled and they picked it up and ran it in.

It's tough to come back against a team like the Packers when you spot them 14 points. But we could have easily won that game. They were a better team than we were in 1966 because we were still so young and they had guys like Jerry Kramer and Ray Nitschke and Bart Starr who had played in the NFL longer than the Dallas Cowboys had been an NFL franchise. But still it got to be 34–27 late in the game. We had the ball first and goal on their 2-yard line with less than two minutes to go. If we score, it goes into overtime and anything can happen in overtime. But there was a holding penalty and then a dropped pass and the rest, as they say, is history.

So that defeat stuck in our craw and the next year we met them again for the NFL title. But this time the game was in Green Bay.

Everybody always asks me, "How cold was it that day? How cold was the Ice Bowl?" I'll tell you how cold it was. It was the coldest day ever recorded in Green Bay history. Not just the coldest December 31 on record. The coldest day *ever*!

Now we're not talking here about the coldest day ever recorded in Dallas or Phoenix or some place like that. We're talking about Green Bay, Wisconsin. God's answer to the walk-in freezer. It got to be 18 degrees below zero that day, podner. The windchill factor brought it down to 57 below. That's 89 degrees below freezing!

On the day before the game we practiced on Lambeau Field and it was actually pretty nice. It was 15 degrees above zero, the sun was shining and after you worked up a good sweat, it felt great. It wasn't a day you'd go sunbathing but for football it was perfect. The field was in good shape too. Lombardi had installed heat coils in the turf to keep the field from freezing over.

The forecast for the next day was for more of the same, so we went to bed ready to play for the championship. When Reeves and I woke up the next day, we got dressed and walked out the door to go to the pregame meal. And the cold hit us in the face like a frying pan. Stopped us right in our tracks and we turned around and went back in and got on our overcoats and bundled up. Then we went back out again. It was only fifty yards to the restaurant and by the time we got there, we were frozen all the way through.

We walked in and Reeves said to the waitress, "Boy, it's cold out there."

"Well, it oughta be," she said. "It's seventeen below."

We thought she was kidding. "Sure it is."

"No, I'm serious. It's seventeen below zero and it's supposed to get colder."

The temperature had dropped 32 degrees overnight.

Now I'd never been in cold weather. I thought when it got to freezing it didn't matter how much colder it got. Freezin is freezin. Wrong. Every degree it dropped was painful. From 15 to 17 below was like going from 100 to 60. Every degree is accentuated at those extremes.

Man, it was cold! The official blew the whistle on the first play but it was one of those metal whistles and when he pulled it out of his mouth, it peeled the skin right off his lip. They had to call time out and go in and find some plastic whistles and a new lip for the ref.

Early in the game Reeves got hit in the face and the blow broke his face mask and his upper teeth got knocked through his top lip. And it didn't bleed. Finally he came out and stood over by the heater while they fixed his helmet and he started to warm up a bit. Well, his circulation started to working again and the blood just started gushing out all over his uniform. This was ten minutes after he got hit.

Now that's cold.

The field was exactly like playing on an ice rink. I mean literally. It was one big solid piece of ice. You couldn't stand up much less run and cut. Guys would be standing on the sidelines minding their own business and they'd shift their feet and the next thing they knew, they were on their ass.

I was sitting next to Perkins on the bench and I said, "We must be crazy to be out here playing."

"We're not crazy," he said. "Look behind you. There's about fifty thousand crazy sonuvabitches up there. They paid to come out here and freeze to death."

In the end, it turned out to be an exciting football game though. It was a close, defensive struggle. They dominated the game early, going ahead 14–0, just like they had the previous year. Then George Andrie picked up a fumble and ran it in and that got us started, 14–7. A little later Packer Willie Wood fumbled a punt return at their 17 and Villanueva kicked a field goal and we went in trailing 14–10 at the half.

Nobody did a thing in the third quarter. Then, on the first play of the fourth quarter Reeves threw a halfback option pass for a TD that put us ahead. Between quarters Meredith had come up to Dan and said, "What about the halfback pass?" We'd been running the quick pitch a lot and their safeties were really coming up to stop it. That left somebody open downfield.

So Reeves kept his hands down in his jock through the quarter to keep his hands warm. And when they broke the huddle to run that play, Reeves kept them right next to his jewels, probably the warmest place in Green Bay that day.

He took his hands out of his jock at the last second and it worked. Reeves lofted a pass to a wide-open Lance Rentzel and he waltzed untouched into the end zone. And we led 17–14.

On the next series Green Bay went nowhere and then we kept the ball for ten minutes on a long drive. When the Packers finally got the ball back, they were on their 32-yard line with four and a half minutes to play. No one thought they had a chance to drive the length of the field in that weather. But they did.

They moved steadily downfield to our 30. Then Chuck Howley slipped and went down covering Chuck Mercein and, just like that, they were down to our 11. Three plays later they were on our 2-yard line, first and goal. They tried a couple off-tackle plays and got nowhere. With sixteen seconds left in the game, still trailing by 3, they took their last timeout.

So everybody figured with no timeouts they'd probably go for a field goal to tie the game. Or they could try a pass into the end zone and if it was incomplete, the clock would stop and they could kick the field goal then. But a run didn't figure at all. If they don't make it, the game's over and we win.

A quarterback sneak by Bart Starr is just not the smart play. So that's what they do and he scores to win the game.

And Jerry Kramer writes a book called *Instant Replay* about
how he made the key block on Jethro Pugh and it turns out
to be the best-selling football book of all time and it makes
Kramer famous and a million dollars. And we lose another
heartbreaker.

If Dallas had won both those games, and we could have
easily, then Landry would have been proclaimed a genius
even sooner. If Bart Starr doesn't score, if Jethro Pugh stuffs
Kramer, then Jethro could have written the best seller. If, if,
if. . . .

But like Meredith used to say, "If ifs and buts were
candies and nuts, we'd all have a Merry Christmas."

Oh, they went bananas trying to figure out why we
couldn't win the Big One. Coach Landry hired a shrink to
make up a questionnaire asking each player what he thought
was wrong with the team. Why hadn't we been able to win
it all? Everybody was searching for an answer.

Then a little thing called the player draft solved everything. In 1969 Roger Staubach and Calvin Hill joined the
team. Then in 1970 we got Duane Thomas, Charlie Waters,
Cliff Harris, John Fitzgerald and Pat Toomay in the draft.
And just like that we were ready to win the Big One. It's
amazing what a bunch of good players can do for a team.

When Roger Staubach joined the Cowboys in 1969 as a
twenty-seven-year-old rookie, nobody figured he'd do much
of anything. Yeah, he'd been the Heisman Trophy winner at
the Naval Academy. But that was way back in 1963. The
Cowboys had drafted him in the tenth round of the 1965 draft
on a longshot that in five years, when Roger's tour of duty
was up, he'd be both willing and able to play in the NFL.

But Roger Staubach, of course, was a different kind of
person than your normal *Homo sapiens.* He'd be out on a

destroyer in the Gulf of Tonkin or some ungodly place for nine months at a time and then he'd take his leave and come to training camp and work out! That's how sick he was. We'd see him out there sweating his ass off through two-a-days and we'd say, "What in the hell is he doin here? He can't even play for three, four more years."

The guy had been off serving his country for eleven months and he gets three weeks off and he's out there every day working his butt off. Training camp is exactly like going to boot camp all over again. In fact, I've been to both boot camp and training camp and I'd rather go to boot camp. But Roger'd be out there with us every year.

Now you've got to admire that kind of dedication. The principles Roger stood for, he wouldn't waver from. If a guy won't compromise his beliefs, no matter what they are, you gotta respect him.

Roger is not a hypocrite. He don't say, "Hey, you oughta do this." And then he does something else. Roger just says, "This is what I do." He don't try to tell you what you oughta do. He ain't a bit phony.

One thing about Roger Staubach, I've always respected him. I always will. I don't want to spend a lot of time with him but I sure do respect his ass.

See, Roger just wasn't given to having a good time. He's against having fun. It's in his genes or something. Anything that's fun, you're not supposed to do. That's the way he feels.

One time somebody said, "Boy, wouldn't you love to have your kid grow up to be more like Roger Staubach?"

And Meredith said, "No way. I'd want my kid to have more fun."

That's the way I feel about Roger. I could never figure out why he couldn't loosen up and have more fun.

My wife and I had a party up at our place one year and we invited a bunch of the Cowboys and I called Roger and he said, "Oh, ya, we'll be there." Then he called back about a day before the party and said he had to go away on business.

Next year, same deal. I invited everybody and Roger calls again the day before the party and says, "Oh, Walt, I'm sorry. I'll be out of town."

"Roger," I said, "nobody gives a shit if you come. You're not the life of the goddamn party anyway. I'll bet tomorrow night not one sonuvabitch at that party will come up to me and say, 'I wonder where Roger is. It just ain't the same without him.' So don't feel bad about it, Roger."

Staubach tried to be one of the guys but it just wasn't in him. Every time he tried, it backfired on him.

For some reason I was sort of his nemesis.

I got Roger to try snuff once. Only I forgot to tell him you've got to spit. Roger swallowed. Now, I don't know if you've ever been sick on tobacco but anybody who has knows it's a bad sick. Your hair starts sweating.

Roger was chewing at a team meeting. He sat there awhile and pretty soon his whole body kinda turned green on him. Then he got up right in the middle of the meeting and went outside and puked his guts out in some rose bushes and came back in and sat down. About five minutes later he gets back up and he's out in the rose bushes again. Then, he went back to his room and didn't come out for thirty-six hours. He ended up missing two days of practice. That was a first for Roger and he never forgave himself. Or me.

But Roger kept trying to fit in and have fun—no matter how much it hurt. On the last day of training camp every year the defense and offense scrimmage each other. After the scrimmage they throw a party for the veterans. The veterans go out to a nice restaurant and the team actually pays for it. Steaks and a lot of booze.

Anyway, Roger's first year with the team we invited him to come with us even though, technically, he was a rookie. Hell, he'd been to five training camps already. So he goes. Now, on Saturday night, rookies have to be in by eleven. But the veterans can stay out until midnight. So we're down there bullshittin and drinking and carrying on and Roger says, "Gosh darn, I've got to be going. I've got to be in by eleven."

And I say, "Hell, you don't have to be in by eleven. You're with the veterans. Hell, you're a veteran now."

So, of course, Roger bought it and when he came in at twelve with the rest of us, Landry fined him $150.

Another time we were at practice shortly after my wife and I had just had our first son. And Roger said, "I don't know, gosh darn, my wife and I have had four kids and they've all been girls. And the first one you have is a boy. How did you do it, Walt?"

"Well," I said, "I really can't explain it, Roger. But I'll tell you what, if you bring Mary Ann by the house I'll try and getcha one."

He was pissed off at me for five years about that crack. Seemed innocent enough to me. Just trying to help out a friend any way I could.

The funny thing is I told his wife and she thought it was funny as hell. I just love Mary Ann. She's the one who keeps Roger human, I think. She'll have a glass of wine or two and laugh at your crude jokes and just relax. Not Roger. Even when he's laughing, he's at attention.

Coach Landry's wife, Alicia, is the same way as Roger's wife. She's a great gal. Loose and friendly and loves to laugh. She's funny too. A lot funnier than her husband.

Every year at training camp the rookies get their chance to roast and make fun of the coaches and veterans. It's called "The Rookie Show." When Reeves was a rookie they put on a show and at the end, Dan mooned the audience. They opened the curtains and he stuck his redneck ass out there. What he didn't know was that Coach Landry's wife was sitting out in the audience. The Rookie Show is usually strictly no women allowed but this time Alicia came. After the show Alicia walked up to Dan and said, "I really enjoyed the closing number, Dan."

That embarrassed poor Reeves, a good Southern boy. "God, here I am a free agent hoping they'd find a place for me anywhere on the team. And here I am exposing my bare ass to the coach's wife. I'll be gone tomorrow. They'll kiss my sorry ass goodbye."

But they didn't. It just shows you can drink, you can lie, you can drop your drawers in front of the coach's wife but if you can run that football, there's a place for you.

But I wasn't the only one who could muss up Roger's feathers. There was also Billy Parks.

Billy Parks was one of the best receivers we ever had—just a great pair of hands. He could catch anything you threw at him with one hand. Roger loved to throw to Billy. But that's where the love ended.

Parks was from California and he had been soaked in the counterculture. When he took off his helmet this huge mop of frizzy brown hair would explode out of his helmet. He looked just like Harpo Marx but his opinions were just left of Karl Marx.

Parks and Staubach would argue about politics, life, hairdos—anything. Every single day! Staubach would take up for Johnson or Nixon and Parks would bitch about us being in Vietnam. And Staubach's a bad person to bitch to about Vietnam because he spent three, four years there. Parks would stand in front of Roger's locker and they'd go at it. They argued every day about whether Nixon was or wasn't a crook.

Every day. Every single day!

But Parks wouldn't argue with just Roger. He'd argue with anyone. Even Landry. Parks was the one behind "The Great White Shoes Debate."

Nobody had ever questioned Landry's authority. If he said we were gonna wear black shoes, we wore black shoes. But Parks didn't accept that. At the time everybody in the league was wearing white shoes. So Parks says, "Hey, why can't we wear white shoes?" And the big debate was on.

We argued over that for days and finally Landry says, "OK, vote on it. White shoes or black shoes. I'm gonna leave the room and when I come back in I want you to tell me which it is—black or white." So he left the room and we argued and argued.

Lilly said, "I'll never wear white shoes. White shoes are for fags."

We vote and it comes out half for white and half for black.

So Landry comes back in and says, "Well, which is it? Black or white?"

"Half of us want black and half of us want white."

Landry looks around the room with disgust and says, "Ah, wear what you want."

And Billy Parks was a happy man.

Roger Staubach was the epitome of what Landry thought a quarterback should be. He was the most dedicated guy you'll ever be around. If somebody did 100 situps, Roger was going to do 101. If somebody ran a mile in 6 minutes, Roger would do it in 5:59. If somebody threw the ball 60 yards, he was going to throw it 61.

Landry felt that when you've got a guy as dedicated as Roger was, it was very easy to get the other players to go that extra mile to win. Because your leader was out there doing it. Besides that, Roger was a good Christian, went in and served his country and had a great wife and kids.

Landry thought he'd died and gone to heaven.

There was only one little problem. We already had a great quarterback—Craig Morton. And he wasn't gonna just sit back and let this anchor-cranking bastard take his place.

Morton had tremendous physical talents and a great football mind. He could throw the football 70 yards flat-footed and he could read defenses like you read a book. And Craig would play with pain.

But Craig Morton, like Don Meredith before him, was a party animal. In fact, he was the whole zoo. Meredith was not the kind of guy who would give you the impression that football was the most important thing in his life. He wasn't going to push himself to work hard to be the best. He let his natural talents do his work for him, and if that wasn't going to be enough, to hell with it. To Meredith football and life were separate. And he sure wasn't going to let football interfere with his pursuit of all the world had to offer in the way of life, libation and the pursuit of women.

Morton was like Meredith. Football was not his whole life. He was more dedicated than Meredith but that wasn't saying a lot.

Craig was famous for his partying. That boy could rock 'n roll, let me tell you. He spent money like it was fertilizer and he had a couple thousand head of cattle. And, boy, he had some good-lookin' girlfriends. I don't know any of their names but he'd come to a party and he always had somebody shiny with him. But, hell, he didn't have a wife or family and he was the quarterback for the Dallas Cowboys which was glamorous as hell and he had a big contract, so why not enjoy it?

Morton proved he was a great athlete. You'd have to be great to stay out as many nights as he did and do all the crazy stuff he did and still make practice. The guy was phenomenal.

Now Staubach? Well, two beers was a decadent evening for Roger.

Roger and Craig were opposites on the field too. Morton was your basic pocket passer. He was gonna stay in the pocket and deliver the football regardless of what kind of pass rush they threw at him. Not Roger. At the first sign of pressure, he was gone. He created havoc with defenses with his scrambling ability. Roger the Dodger.

They were both great in their own way. So right away we had a quarterback controversy. The press, the fans, the players, hell, even Landry couldn't figure out who to play.

At the time Roger hadn't made the Hall of Fame yet. He hadn't led us to five Super Bowls. He was just a rookie yet to pass the test. And he was pushing an All-Pro quarterback. You think Landry had a few things to think about?

Even the team was split. The defense liked Roger because he made things happen. But the offensive guys loved Craig. We thought he was a better quarterback. He knew the offense better than Roger. He could read defenses better. He had a better feel for the game and a better arm. And Roger hadn't played professional football for very long, whereas Morton had been playing for six or seven years.

Morton was more regimented in the Landry system. When Staubach first came up, if things didn't go his way he scrambled. He ran everywhere. And Landry didn't like that. And neither did the offense. The offense had confidence that it could score with Landry's system and the players it had. When Staubach took off on one of his runs, it was Roger against the world. Throw out Dallas's Multiple Offense, throw out Speed Inc., throw out Bob Hayes the fastest man in the world, throw out the best blocking line in the business.

Ya, and throw out "I'll getcha four yards" Garrison. It was Roger Staubach versus the NFL.

In the end Landry went with Staubach. But even then he had to use them both.

Morton took us to the Super Bowl in 1970 against Baltimore. Then, in 1971, he lost out to Roger in the great quarterback debate. But Roger got injured midway through the season and Craig took over and led us to the divisional title again. Roger stepped in during the playoffs that year and regained his starting position but Morton was the one who got us there.

It was confusing but it worked like magic.

To complement our passing game we also got two great running backs in the 1969 and 1970 drafts—Calvin Hill and Duane Thomas. As a running back it doesn't make you feel all that secure when they draft a running back number one. Especially when it happens in consecutive years. After we picked up Thomas, Reeves said to me, "They trying to tell us something, Walt?"

"I guess so."

We also drafted two defensive backs in the '70 draft who would eventually become perennial All-Pros—Cliff Harris and Charlie Waters. And in a year or two, we had the best defensive backfield in football to go along with the best linebackers and Lilly, the best lineman God ever created.

Cliff Harris was the kinda guy who would fight hell with a bucket of water. He was so determined the first two or three years in the league, it was scary. You never saw a guy so fanatic to succeed. For his size he was one of the toughest players Dallas ever had. He was All-Pro four times and went to the Pro Bowl six times.

But Charlie and Cliff had a lot of adjusting to do in the NFL. The NFL ain't like Ouachita Baptist, Cliff's alma mater. The first time Charlie and Cliff faced Harold Jackson, the speedy split end for the Rams, he ran by them like they were parked. Lee Roy called that game "The Track Meet."

Cliff and Charlie double-teamed Jackson. Then they played inside and outside of him. Then they tried to cripple him. Everything and anything to stop him. And Jackson would just run straight down the field 90 mph. And Cliff would be yelling, "Hey Charlie, he's yours." And Charlie would be yelling, "You got him, Cliff."

After one long Jackson reception, Cliff and Charlie came back in the huddle and Lee Roy says, "What the hell's going on? You gotta stop him. You guys got that bastard double-covered and you still can't cover him. And the rest of us are working our asses off trying to cover the rest of their receivers."

Jackson ended up with four touchdowns on seven receptions for 238 yards.

Cliff was really responsible for two or three of those touchdowns but since they went over Charlie's head it looked like he'd missed his coverage again. So Cliff would come running up to Charlie while he was standing in the end zone and Cliff'd start pointing at the receiver and then at Charlie and he'd be screaming, "I'm sorry, Charlie. I messed up. I shoulda been there."

And the announcer is saying, "Well, it's obvious that Cliff Harris is chewing out Charlie Waters for messing up the coverage again."

And there's Cliff, "I'm sorry! I shoulda been there!" And the fans are all over Charlie. That goddamn Waters missed his assignment again.

Cliff was a smart boy.

The greatest thing that ever happened to Charlie was moving him to strong safety. See, Waters was just too slow to cover a speedy wide receiver at cornerback. He got his ass beat legitimately time after time. Charlie could only cover the short zone, so he'd look for a square out every time. If they went long, he was dead. So, after Cornell Green retired, Landry got wise and moved Charlie to safety and he was All-Pro a couple of times.

Charlie's nemesis his whole career was Charley Taylor of the Redskins. In six games Taylor caught sixteen passes and scored four touchdowns against Charlie. After one particularly bad game, Waters asked Billy Kilmer, the Redskins quarterback, why he didn't throw it toward him on every down.

"I was afraid they were gonna take you out of the game. And we needed you in there," Kilmer said.

That was also the game when Waters broke his arm. Charlie and Cliff went back to cover a punt and Cliff says, "Charlie, we're losing this ball game bad. We've got to do something to get the team fired up. I'll tell you what let's do. Let's run this punt back no matter what. No fair catches no matter where it is."

So they kick it real high and the ball's coming down and Cliff looks up at the ball and then looks downfield and there's three or four Redskins right on top of them. So Cliff yells, "You take it, Charlie! You take it!"

Well, Charlie had gotten beaten for a TD by Taylor just before that, so he takes it. And they broke his arm in about forty places.

They're taking him off the field and Cliff's in tears. "I'm sorry, Charlie. I'm sorry. That was my ball."

"That's OK," Charlie says, "At least, I don't have to cover Taylor anymore."

CHAPTER SIXTEEN

WINNING THE BIG ONE

Another big addition to our team was All-Pro tight end Mike Ditka. We got him in a trade with Philadelphia prior to the '70 season and Mike brought a ferocious, never-give-an-inch competitiveness that sparked the team to fight in every game. Plus, he could catch a football.

Ditka weighed about 235 when he played with us. That's how he got the nickname "Monk." Short for Chipmunk. He had these big ol fat jowls. When he began coaching he started running and lost a lot of weight so he weighs maybe 190 now. But when he played for us, he was a healthy boy. And most of it was around his cheeks and jowls.

Ditka wasn't too fast though and he had no moves at all. Charlie Waters and Cliff Harris used to give Ditka all kinds of crap about his big moves.

"Ya, Mike, you got some great moves." And they'd swivel their heads back and forth. That was the extent of Ditka's moves.

In practice Charlie and Cliff would cover Monk like

paint. They'd be all over him because he couldn't beat them deep and they knew it. So they didn't have to be honest.

Ditka would try his damndest when he was running his routes to get those two little bastards up close enough so he could give them a forearm to the chops. Right before he made his cut, he'd try to cream our cornerbacks.

That was Ditka.

I was happy as hell when Ditka came down to play with us because he was a tough sonuvabitch. He was the kind of guy if there was a brick wall in front of him and he could walk just ten feet down and go around it, he'd say, "Fuck it!" and try and run right through it.

Ditka got his teeth knocked out in an auto accident the year he joined us. He flipped his car up over on top of a parked car. Went through the windshield and broke his jaw.

The dentist told Ditka, "We can wire your teeth shut but you can't play tomorrow. Or we can pull them."

Ditka says, "Pull the sonsabitches."

Well, as it turned out, they had to wire his mouth shut anyway because his jaw was broke. But he played all the same. You could hear him out on the field breathing through his teeth, "hiss-haw, hiss-haw, hiss-haw." Sounded like a rabid hound. And you could hear that mad dog Ditka cussin even with his mouth wired shut. "God da otherucker!"

Man, that Ditka was mean. He walked into a restaurant one night, walked over to a table with some chairs stacked on it and just raked them all off with his big ol forearm and motioned for us to come on over and sit down.

Nobody said a word. I know why too. Ditka had the foulest temper of any man I've ever met. It was so bad people used to like to get him mad just to see what he'd do because he could lose control in a slim second and anything could happen. That was the fun of it—the element of surprise.

I used to go golfing with Ditka and Reeves and Dave Edwards. Mike threw his club after about every shot. He used to throw stuff all over. Hell, I'd just started playing golf and I thought it was part of the game. Get mad, throw a club, cuss, beat your club on the ground, break the damn thing, throw it in the lake. I thought that's how you played golf.

Monk'd throw a club over in the woods and me and Fuzzy'd go on over there and get it and put it in our bags. That's how I got my first set of clubs.

Reeves and Manders played Landry and Ditka in tennis one evening at training camp over at the apartments at Cal Lutheran and there's a lot of young couples there with kids. Everything's real nice and sociable until Ditka gets behind. Then Mike starts up, "Shit! How did I miss that goddamn shot! I hate this fucking game!" At the top of his lungs with mothers scattering trying to get their kids out of earshot. They might as well have moved them to Arizona as loud as Ditka was cussin. "Goddamn sonsabitches!"

The whole time Landry never said a word. Finally, Ditka misses a shot, slams his racket down, smashes it all to hell and throws what's left of it at the net. Well, the damn thing goes *under* the net and skips along the court and hits Landry in the ankles. Tom's hopping around hurting like hell and he looks over at Reeves and says, "Boy, you can get hurt playing *this* game."

Ya, Ditka was a madman. When we were all into motorcycles, Mike bought a Yamaha. It was yellow but that didn't fit Mike's image of himself. So he painted it black and he bought a black leather jacket and black leather pants and a black helmet. Man, he looked like Lucifer on wheels.

Only problem was he couldn't ride worth beans. One place we used to go riding a lot had a hill with a creek at the bottom and Monk'd always try to jump the creek. And every time he'd miss and hit the other bank. Bam! "Goddamn it!"

And he'd start that thing up again, go back and try to jump it again and he'd miss again. Bam! "Goddamn it!" He'd get up and go again. Bam! "Goddamn it!"

But what really pissed Ditka off was Cliff and Charlie could hop that creek like it was a puddle. And they'd yell back at Mike, "Come on, you fat chipmunk!" And ride off. Ditka hated those two little bastards. So he'd go back and Bam! "Goddamn it!"

After the Super Bowl one year a bunch of Cowboys went up skiing in Vail. There were about eight couples—Ditka, Manders, Reeves, Lee Roy and myself among them.

Well, Ditka can't ski for shit but, of course, that don't mean nothing to Mike. Full speed ahead even if you don't know what you're doing. The rest of us were all pretty good skiers so we took the chair lift to the top of the mountain and Ditka comes right along with us. His wife Marge went along too. She had on a purple outfit that musta cost her a couple grand, at least. Oh, man, she had on purple pants, purple boots, a purple jacket, a purple hat. And a blond wig. She looked sensational!

Well, she came off that chair lift at the top and it was all iced over up there and *ppsssssssssst*! She flew right off that mountain and rolled over and over a few times and her blond wig and purple hat flew right off and rolled a couple hundred feet down the mountain.

While the rest of us picked her up, Mike takes off. She was really pissed. We're all asking how she was and her husband's skiing off in the other direction. Couldn't care less. Hey, he had a job to do. He had to conquer that goddamn mountain.

Mike likes to dress well. He had on a sweater that day that probably cost him $300. Well, it took Mike about an hour to ski down that hill. He'd ski across and fall. Then he'd get up and cuss awhile and then he'd ski across and fall and cuss some more. And by the time he got down to the bottom, he had fallen so many times his sweater was soaked and it had stretched all the way down to his knees. It looked like a trench coat and he looked like a walrus. He had snot and ice all frozen in his moustache and he was sweating like a bull on mating day. I mean this mother was hot!

Well, I figured Mike was so miserable that when we finally got him down, all he'd want to do is go in the lodge and drink. Wrong. Not Ditka. He gets down to the bottom of the slope, takes one final head-over-ashcan fall, gets up and says, "Let's go again!"

A few years later, we were playing St. Louis at Texas Stadium and he was special-teams coach that year. The officials were flagging Mike's guys all day long. And Ditka was stomping and cussin and fuming all along the sidelines. Finally, the officials told him he better take it easy or he's gone.

Well, it got to be the fourth quarter and they flagged his team one more time. This time for off-sides. Ditka went out on the field and he was real calm and he says to the official, "Excuse me, sir. Are you a member of the Fellowship of Christian Athletes?"

The official kind of looks at him like, huh? "No."

"Well, then fuck you!"

Landry just melted on the sidelines. They took Ditka away after that.

Ditka's legendary temper really got a workout when we played cards. It was always a circus when Mike would play. First of all, he's the worst card player in the world. Secondly, he hates to lose. And thirdly, he's got that goddamn temper. Put them all together, you got pandemonium Ditka-style.

We'd usually play a card game called boo-ray before a game and, of course, Monk'd lose his ass, and he'd get so mad he'd start throwing chairs across the room. Hell, Ditka was throwing chairs when Bobby Knight over at Indiana

University was still using his to sit in. His big ol chipmunk cheeks would turn red. Then Ditka'd take the deck of cards and tear them in half and throw the sonuvabitches in the air like confetti.

And Lee Roy'd say, "Well, it looks like the game's over."

"Goddamn game ain't over till I get a chance to win this goddamn money back," Ditka would scream.

"Whatever you say, Monk."

You're probably wondering why the hell we let him play. Well, the thing about Ditka was if you just played cards long enough with him, he'd get mad and give you all his money. Before he'd destroy the game, he'd hand you every cent he had. So everybody loved it when Monk played.

Ditka would stay in a hand and try to beat you when he had nothing. And everybody knew it. He was so competitive he wanted to win even if he had an eight-high nothin. As soon as he got pissed off, he'd bet and bet no matter what he had. And we all knew it. It was like having your own automated teller window.

All you could hear through the halls at night was Ditka screaming, "Ah, shit!" "Goddamnit!" And you knew Monk was losing again.

They played mostly for markers in camp. "You owe me three hundred dollars." "OK, here's my marker for three hundred." Then at the end of camp they'd settle up.

Well, by the end of camp, Ditka didn't have no money, of course. And he owed thousands. There was no way he could pay it all. He owed this guy $1200, that guy $1500, another guy $2000. And so he'd go up to each guy and say, "How much on a dollar would you like? Twenty cents on the dollar? I mean, how much actual cash will you take for what I owe you? No way I can pay twelve hundred."

The funny thing is nobody was really pissed off. The money came so easy from Monk, if they got twenty cents on the dollar it was easier than winning straight from somebody else.

Lee Roy was the only one really upset about the transactions. Lee Roy was smart. He wouldn't drink and he'd just sit there and play his cards and everybody else was drunk as hell, screaming and yelling, laughing and swearing. And, of course, Lee Roy was eatin em up.

Buddy Dial was out a grand to Lee Roy, Howley owed him a bunch, and Monk, of course, had signed over his mortgage and his first-born child.

The gambling got so bad that when it came time for the first exhibition game, players were more concerned about who was going to get cut and leave without paying than they were about the team. Guys'd be trying to make another player look good just so Landry wouldn't cut his ass and take their winnings with him.

"What happened to Thomas?"

"The Turk got him."

"Shit, there goes my eight hundred bucks."

Well, Landry got pissed off one time about the gambling so he gets up in a meeting and says, "No more cards. No more gambling. It's disrupting the team."

So we all went back to our rooms after the meeting and we decided, well, nobody would get a chance to win any money back so all bets were off. We were gonna just tear up all the "owsies."

Lee Roy tore up $5,000 or $6,000 worth of IOU's. And five days later the sonuvabitches were playing again. Why not? They suddenly had all this money saved up that they hadn't lost yet.

As you might expect, Meredith was the best card player on the team. He was so cool he could bluff you into the deep freeze even if you had a full house looking back at you. I stayed clear of any game Meredith was in. One sniff would cost me $500. Besides, when I was first with the Cowboys, I didn't have the kind of money Meredith had. Hell, I never had the kind of money Joe Don had. Still don't.

When I was a rookie Jimmy Saddle, a number-two draft choice from Auburn, used to come down to Meredith's room and play gin. And Don would beat the bejesus out of Saddle every night. Saddle was a rich kid and he'd hand over two, three thousand a night to Meredith! I ain't kiddin. Meredith was vicious.

I seen him out there when the players would get their per diem checks at camp. You know, maybe three, four hundred dollars. And Joe Don and two other guys would flip for the checks. Odd man out. And the winner would get all three checks. Just like that.

Hell, in my rookie year those per diem checks were the largest paycheck I'd ever gotten in my life. I used to keep fifty bucks and send the rest back to Mother. Hell, I thought those were my salary checks. Until the season started and I got my first regular check. Those checks were so big I thought it was a loan or something.

With the addition of all those great players, we were a much better team when the 1970 season started and we won the conference going away with a 10–4 record. But it wasn't easy. We were 3–3 when we faced St. Louis on a Monday night midway through the season. We were supposed to handle the Cardinals easily and they killed us 38–0.

We hit bottom then and Landry let off a little on us. Instead of coming in and lifting weights after drills, we started playing touch football at practice. And suddenly we were having fun again. I'm not sure if the coaches had given up on us or what.

I'm not a psychologist. I don't know what makes a team play better but we sure did that year after Landry decided to play it a little more relaxed. Up to the St. Louis game we were having trouble doing anything right, and after the game we couldn't do anything wrong. Everybody went into the games more relaxed and we won. Then we won again and again. And winning breeds winning and pretty soon we'd won nine straight games and we were in the Super Bowl.

The Super Bowl was a nightmare for us. We played Baltimore and before it was all over they called it the Blooper Bowl. There were five fumbles, six interceptions and enough weird plays to last a season. And that was from the two teams that were supposed to be the best in football.

The outcome hinged on two strange and controversial plays. First Earl Morrall, the aging Baltimore quarterback who came in when Unitas was knocked out in the first quarter by George Andrie, threw a pass to Eddie Hinton. But Mel Renfro was all over Hinton like a cheap suit. The ball went off Hinton and landed in the hands of Colt John Mackey and Mackey walked into the end zone for an 80-yard score to tie the game. The only problem with that play is it's illegal. A defensive man must touch the ball before another offensive player can catch a tipped pass. If you look at the films, the last person you can see touch the ball before Mackey was Hinton. But the officials ruled that Renfro had touched it. Mel swears to this day he never did.

Then in the third quarter we were leading 13–6 and had driven down to the 2-yard line. We were about to apply the knockout punch to the Colts. The handoff went to Duane and he fumbled the ball. No problem. Dave Manders was all over the ball and recovered it.

But Billy Ray Smith of the Colts yelled, "Our ball! Our ball!" and he jumped up and down, really giving it the Oscar-nominee performance. And they bought it. Without even unpiling the players, they signaled that it was the Colts' ball.

"It rolled right under me and I fell on it," Manders said. "I got up and handed the ball to the ref with a big smile on my face. I couldn't believe it when they gave it to Baltimore. I still can't believe it."

And that was that. If we scored there, it would have made it 20–6 and the game is over. But it wasn't.

The last disaster that day happened late in the game. The game was tied 13–13 and we were driving for a score. We had the ball on the Baltimore 27, ready to put it away with a field goal when Morton flipped a pass a little high out to Reeves and he tipped the ball into the air and Mike Curtis intercepted it and ran it back to our 28. A couple plays later Jim O'Brien trotted out onto the field and kicked a field goal to beat us 16–13.

It was a close game but we lost. Close only counts in horseshoes, hand grenades and dancin. And just like that the press was saying all over again that we couldn't win The Big One.

Geez!

I really believe we had a better team than Baltimore in 1970 but the big game for us that year was when we finally beat San Francisco to *get* to the Super Bowl. We were much more intense for that game than we were for the Colts. Nobody said, "Hey, we're gonna kill these guys." It was just a relief to finally get to the Super Bowl because we'd come so close the previous four years and never made it.

But, in 1971, from the first day of training camp, our entire team was dedicated to winning the Super Bowl. We knew we could do it. We knew we were the best team in football and we went out and proved it. We breezed through the season. We won the last ten games of the year and beat

Minnesota and San Francisco in the playoffs to go back to the Super Bowl where we all felt we belonged.

The important factor for us in winning Super Bowl VI was that we'd been there before. We knew what to expect. Very few teams have gone to the Super Bowl for the first time and won it. And that's no accident.

The first time a team goes to a Super Bowl they're just like a goose. They wake up in a new world every day. There's nine million reporters and cameras and people shoving microphones in your face. That hype is powerful stuff. There are people around your hotel all the time and every one of them wants to be near you and give you whatever you want—and a lot of those people are pretty women.

You really can't handle it all the first time out. Your mind is on the people, the excitement, the chaos, the hoopla of the whole extravaganza. Everywhere except the game. Oh, you think you're concentrating on the game but you're not really and you don't realize it until you come back a second time and remember how you acted, how you felt. The first time you play in a Super Bowl, the game is like a dream and you end up doing a lot of sleepwalking through it.

When we showed up in New Orleans in 1971 we knew what to expect. We knew every reporter in the Western Hemisphere would be there. We knew we'd have to spend one to two hours a day in the press room. So it didn't bother us. We knew it was going to be a zoo. It wasn't unexpected anymore. It was expected. And that definitely helped us win.

The game was all business for us. There wasn't a lot of screaming and hollering in the locker room. We just took care of business.

The Dolphins had a great young team that year. In fact, they went on to be one of the great teams of all time. In 1972 they posted a perfect 17–0 season and went on to win two consecutive Super Bowls.

They had Jim Kiick and Larry Csonka and Bob Griese in the backfield and their defense was a swarming aggressive unit headed by Nick Buoniconti, Jake Scott and Manny Fernandez. But they were still young in 1971 and our experience was too much for them.

Our game plan was to key on Buoniconti because he controlled their defense. We started out giving the ball to me and running inside. If Nick floated outside on the play, I'd cut back. If he stayed in the middle, I'd go off the tight end. I just keyed on him. At halftime they adjusted to what we were doing, so then we faked the ball to me and pitched it to Duane and he ran wild outside.

That was probably the most perfect football game I've ever played in. We did nothing wrong. The defense stopped them cold and the offense did whatever it wanted. We won 24–3 and it wasn't that close. With a minute to go Calvin Hill fumbled as he was crossing the goal line or it would have been 31–3.

Duane and I ended up setting a Super Bowl record for most yards gained with 252 and Roger was voted the Most Valuable Player.

The scene in the locker room after the victory was different than you'd expect. Nobody got stinking drunk and poured champagne all over everyone or threw Landry in the shower or tried to pants the TV guys. The feeling was one of relief. We'd finally done it. Oh, there was some hootin and hollerin but nobody went out of their minds crazy.

We were a great team who'd had a great season and played like we were supposed to in the Super Bowl. Sitting in the locker room with a bottle of champagne, ripping tape off my arms, I looked over at Lilly and I knew he was thinking what I was thinking, "Thank God, we've done it!"

They could say anything they wanted now. Except they couldn't say, "Dallas can't win the Big One."

CHAPTER SEVENTEEN

STILL A COWBOY

After the 1974 season, I retired. I was only thirty but thirty is a grandpa for a running back in the National Football League. A running back takes a hell of a beating on every play. And though nobody likes to admit it, you lose a step as you get older. You're just a tiny bit slower and in football that tiny bit is everything.

The holes suddenly have to be bigger for you to get through them. The smaller ones you used to get through close up faster than a whorehouse during an election.

Also, I didn't want to get cut. I wanted to retire on my own. I didn't want to be like George Blanda. He played for twenty-six years and they finally cut him when he was forty-six or forty-seven. "For God's sake, George, go home!" That wasn't for me.

I didn't have a big press conference or nothing. I called Coach Landry and told him, "I'm done." And that was it.

I played nine years and I could still walk relatively well and U.S. Tobacco offered me a full-time position in their

Special Events Department. It was a very old company with a lot of young people at the top with young ideas about selling chewing tobacco. So I thought I had a great opportunity to get into something that was gonna last a lot longer than nine years. I couldn't see holding on to a career that was coming to an end when a great opportunity was staring me in the face. So part of my retiring was strictly a business decision.

So I retired and I've never looked back.

I really enjoyed playing football. I used to look forward to Sunday like you look forward to a big party. I loved it. There ain't nothing like a Sunday from the time you wake up until the time the game's over. The dopeheads can take whatever they want but they'll never get that kind of high.

The closest I've ever come to it is the rodeo arena. Steer wrestlin at the Cheyenne Rodeo—"The Granddaddy of Rodeos." Now I've been to the Indy 500 and I'm sure those drivers get that kind of high. Or baseball players at the World Series. Or a skier at the Olympics. The crowds, the competition, the thrill of knowing you're the best at something and performing it in front of sixty thousand people. Every Sunday I got an unbelievable feeling of life being lived at full throttle.

But I've never looked back and said, "God, I wish I was still playing." I've never thought that way. That's like saying, "I wish I was still in high school. I was so good-lookin then." I don't wish I was still in high school and I don't wish I was still playing for the Dallas Cowboys.

Now take a guy like Roger. Roger was a great athlete. And he still is. He lifts weights and he works out religiously. He still wants to play basketball and touch football all the time. Anytime you want to have a touch football game, call Roger, he'll get one together for you. I don't think he's ever got it out of his blood.

But I just don't think you can go back and relive the past. If you show up in the old locker room, you ain't gonna relive anything except the smell of a bunch of old sweaty socks.

Actually, I follow Denver now more than Dallas because I gotta pull for Reeves. Dan invited me and Lee Roy and Manders up for a game last year when Frog's team played the Cowboys up in Denver. But I couldn't make it, so I watched it on TV from New York and there was Jordan and Manders down on the Denver sidelines. Now Lee Roy is a fanatic Cowboys fan. He goes to every game and lives and dies with the team but he was over there cheering for Frog to get to the Super Bowl. And I woulda been right there with him.

When I first started working for Skoal, Lou Bantle, the chairman of the board, called me and said, "What would you think about moving near the corporate headquarters here in Connecticut?"

"I think I need to find me another job," I said. "Mr. Bantle, if you've got it in your mind that somewhere down the road I'm going to move to Connecticut, please tell me now, because I ain't moving to Connecticut."

"Why not?" he says. "You could move up in the company faster."

"Mr. Bantle, the one thing I've got going for U.S. Tobacco is my enthusiasm. I like what I do. Now you're trying to take even that away from me. You take me away from Texas, you take away my enthusiasm."

See, I'm still basically the same person I always was. Just a small-town kid from Texas. At home inside my shirt. I grew up in Lewisville and I guess I'll die here.

Awhile back I bought the old Liberty Theater on Main Street in Lewisville and I converted it into a Skoal office and that's where I work. I got twenty-three acres out in Argyle just up the road from Lewisville. I'm living over a barn. My horses are underneath. My wife's at my side. My boys are doin good. Life ain't too bad.

I'm happier than I've ever been. I've been married since 1986 to my second wife, Debbie, a former Miss Rodeo America. The beer joints aren't as important to me now as they used to be. I go down and brush my horses instead of brushing one of those barmaids. Some of those gals need a lot of brushing too.

Like Charlie Waters said the other day, "I'm probably getting boring now."

No, I ain't changed all that much. I'm forty-three years old and I still wear blue jeans, cowboy boots and a western hat. I still enjoy being around horses and I still ride every day. I still like to whittle and drink a beer and sit and bullshit with nice people.

Walt Garrison is still just a cowboy from a small town in Texas who played for the Dallas Cowboys and enjoys the memories.

ABOUT THE AUTHORS

WALT GARRISON now lives in Lewisville, Texas, with his wife, Debbie, a former Miss Rodeo America, and his two teenage sons.

★★★★★

JOHN TULLIUS lives in California. He has written scores of articles on sports and other subjects and is the author of several books, including the oral history of the New York Yankees, *I'd Rather Be a Yankee.*